Dark & Dramatic
Mosaic Crochet

A Master Guide to Overlay Colorwork
with 15 Modern Goth & Alternative Patterns

Alexis Sixel
Creator of Sixel Design

PAGE STREET
PUBLISHING CO.

PAGE STREET
PUBLISHING CO.

First published in 2023 by
Page Street Publishing Co.
27 Congress Street, Suite 1511
Salem, MA 01970
www.pagestreetpublishing.com

Distributed by Macmillan, sales in Canada by The Canadian Manda Group.

27   26   25   24   23   1 2 3 4 5

ISBN-13: 978-1-64567-911-0
ISBN-10: 1-64567-911-X

Library of Congress Control Number: 2022947318

Cover and book design by Molly Kate Young for Page Street Publishing Co.
Photography by Alexis Sixel

Printed and bound in the United States

To Grandma Dorothy,

Did you ever imagine your rebellious granddaughter would end up just like you, crocheting every single day? I wish I could share this book with you and show you how wild this craft has become! Thank you for passing down the crochet gene. Love you and miss you.

Table of Contents

Introduction

What is this sorcery?

If you're already intimidated by the pictures in this book, let me start off by assuring you that mosaic crochet really is so much easier than it looks!

When I first discovered mosaic crochet a few years ago, the most advanced things I could crochet at the time were granny squares. I had never tried colorwork, and never even heard of the term before! I always thought changing and joining colors while crocheting would be such a hassle, and probably too complicated for a novice like me. Not mosaic crochet! Learning the simplicity of this technique was revolutionary to me, and it opened up a world of creative possibilities that completely reinvigorated my love of crochet. So much so that I haven't been able to put my hook down since!

After learning the basics, I was inspired to try and create designs with different curves and angles by manipulating the placement of the basic stitches. One of the first designs I was determined to make was a skull, which is something I love to collect and have all over my home. It took a bit of experimenting and lots of swatches, but the process of figuring it out and developing a technique with new stitches was so exciting! The skull pattern ended up being a big hit, and it gave me the confidence to continue designing patterns with a goth/alternative edge and to develop even more stitches to stretch the boundaries of mosaic crochet.

I never intended on being a pattern designer—nor did I think crocheting would be such a huge part of my life—but now that I'm here, I wouldn't change it for the world. The best part is being able to share my passion with others, teaching them new techniques and seeing them create amazing works of art with the patterns I write from my couch. It is such a fun, therapeutic and addicting hobby, and I'm happy to be an enabler!

These are the only stitches you'll need to know before starting this book:

- Single crochet
- Double crochet
- Chains
- Slip stitches

It really is that simple. This book will teach you everything else, from the basics of reading charts, to creating curves, angles and points with advanced special stitches. So, grab your favorite hook, some black and neon yarn and let's get started!

Getting Started with Mosaic Crochet

The Basics

Mosaic crochet is an easy colorwork technique for creating intricate patterns without having to change colors in the middle of a row. It uses single crochet (SC) and double crochet (DC) stitches to change the colors in the row below to create complex patterns and designs.

This book will teach you the overlay mosaic crochet technique, and this tutorial will guide you through the basics. You will also learn how to add these stitches in different placements to create curves and angles with special stitches. (See page 163 for full instructions on special stitches.)

Mosaic patterns are created by working all SC stitches into the top back loops of the same row, and dropping down all DC stitches into the front loops of the row below of the same color. This is where the term "overlay" comes from. The DC

Example of an overlay DC stitch

stitches are covering up the SC stitches from the previous row, allowing you to alter the colors in the previous row.

Designs are worked from the front side only, from right to left (or from left to right for left-handed crocheters). Each row alternates between two contrasting colors, either A or B. When following a mosaic crochet chart, the numbered columns on the right and left sides are color coded with the color you will be crocheting the entire row with, either color A or B. **The chart we are using for this tutorial starts with color A (purple) for row 1, and color B (white) for row 2.**

All of these patterns are chart based and are read stitch by stitch in the same direction as you're crocheting. Each box represents 1 stitch. Once you become familiar with how to read charts, it becomes much easier than reading a written pattern because you'll have a visual reference for how each row should look and where all the stitches will line up in each row.

In most mosaic crochet charts, the mosaic design does not start until row 3. You will need to set up 2 foundation rows with all SC stitches, 1 row in color A and 1 row in color B, both worked into the top back loops only. This will give you a foundation to start working your mosaic stitches. You will also be adding a border stitch at the beginning and end of each row to anchor the next color and keep your rows lined up.

Tea House Chart

8 stitches in repeat

10	X	X					X	X	X					X	X	10
9			X			X				X			X			9
8				X	X	X				X	X	X				8
7	X							X							X	7
6				X	X	X				X	X	X				6
5			X			X				X			X			5
4	X	X					X	X	X					X	X	4
3					X						X					3
2																2
1																1

Repeat Section

Color A Color B

Stitch Key

	Single Crochet	All blank boxes SC, top back loop only
X	Double Crochet	DC in the row below of the same color

You will only be reading and following the symbols on each row of the chart (Xs in this pattern), and not changing colors based on the shaded boxes. The shaded boxes in the center of the chart show you what the row below looks like after you've added overlay stitches. So, when you're looking at row 3 of the chart, those white boxes are all of the SC stitches from row 2, and the shaded Xs are overlay stitches you're adding on row 3 to row 2.

This is why some patterns that have rows with no overlay stitches have the opposite color shaded in the middle, but the entire row is crocheted in the other color. **Always use the color indicated in the numbered column of the charts, not the shaded boxes shown in the middle of the chart.**

Foundation Rows

This pattern has 8 stitches in each repeat section **(2 repeats shown in the chart)**, plus 1 stitch at the end of the row. We will make our swatch with 3 repeats so we can also use it later as a gauge swatch.

Each pattern will either list the number of multiples you'll need to calculate your foundation chain, or it will list a specific number of chains to start with.

For this chart, we have multiples of 8 plus 1. We are multiplying the repeat by 3 to make it 3 times wider.

Our foundation chain will be $3 \times 8 + 1 = 25$.

Since this swatch will be crocheted flat with border stitches, we need to add 2 more chains:

$25 + 2 = 27$.

Begin your foundation chain in color A **(outline color)** with 27 chains.

Row 1 will be a row of all SC stitches into the chain.

Chain 1 and SC into the second chain from the hook. SC the entire row to the end. Chain 1, pull down to tighten, cut a 3" (7.6-cm) tail and pull through.

Row 2 will be a row of all SC stitches in color B **(background color)** into the top back loops of row 1, starting and ending with a border stitch.

Border Stitches

1. To make a border stitch, insert your hook into both loops of the first stitch in the row.

Border Stitches (continued)

2. Hook color B, leaving about a 2" to 3" (5- to 7.5-cm) tail, and pull through a loop.

3. Hook the tail and pull it all the way through the loop. **This will secure the tail to the side so you can begin adding a border stitch on top.**

4. Insert your hook back into the loop.

5. Chain 1. Insert your hook back into both loops of the base of the stitch and add 1 SC. **Repeat these steps for adding a border stitch at the beginning of each row.**

Row 2

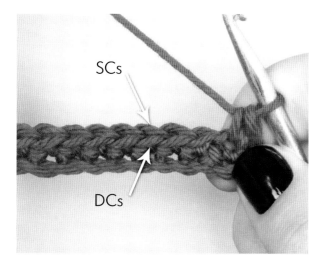

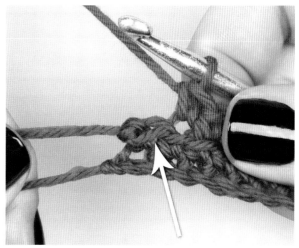

For row 2, add SC stitches into the top back loops only, and stop when you have 1 stitch left.

When looking at the top of the chain, the front loops will be reserved for any overlay DC stitches in the next row, and all SC stitches will be in the top back loops.

In the last stitch of the row you'll add an ending border stitch. Insert your hook into both loops of the last stitch and add a SC. Pull the yarn down to tighten. Chain 1 and pull down to tighten. Cut a 2" to 3" (5- to 7.5-cm) tail and pull through.

All remaining rows will end with a border stitch into both loops of the previous border stitch.

Ending border stitch.

Row 2 complete.

Reading Charts

Looking at the chart, you will be reading each row from right to left. Each box represents a stitch. All DC stitches are marked with an "X" and all SC stitches are blank.

The chart has a repeat section that's 8 stitches across, starting from the first stitch in the row. Some charts may start with stitches before the repeat section, and you will add those before following the stitches in the repeat. This chart also shows 8 stitches repeated again, just so you can see how the pattern lines up. You only need to follow the stitches marked in the repeat section and any stitches at the beginning or end of the row outside the repeat.

For left-handed crocheters reading the chart from left to right, the first stitch is outside the repeat section, so you will add that stitch first before following across the repeat section.

Row 3

DC

Begin row 3 (and all remaining rows) with a border stitch. The first 4 stitches are SC, the 5th stitch is a DC and the next 3 stitches are SC. The DC stitch will be crocheted into the front loop of the row below of the same color.

Here are the first 8 stitches completed in the repeat section. Repeat this sequence 2 more times across the row.

Row 3 completed.

After you've repeated those 8 stitches 3 times, you will see 2 stitches remaining. The next stitch is the last stitch in the row of the chart after the repeat, 1 SC. **For left-handed crocheters, this will be your first stitch.** Finish the row (and all remaining rows) with an ending border stitch in the very last stitch of the row.

Row 4

Row 4 starts with 2 DCs into the front loops of the row below of the same color.

The repeat section for row 4 is 2 DCs, 5 SCs and 1 DC. Repeat this sequence 2 more times across the row, and finish with the last stitch in the row, 1 DC.

Reading Charts (continued)

When you're crocheting DC stitches into the front loops, there will be stitches in the back that do not have any stitches connected to them. For every DC stitch, there will be the same number of blank skipped stitches in the back. **This is very important to pay attention to, especially when you start adding special stitches in more advanced patterns.**

Here we have 3 DC stitches, and 3 skipped stitches in the back. You'll notice that this leaves a little pocket when you have several consecutive DC stitches in a row. This is perfectly normal, and once you have several rows added these pockets are a lot less noticeable.

Row 4 completed.

Row 5

Row 5 starts with 2 SCs, 1 DC, 3 SCs, 1 DC and 1 SC. Repeat this sequence 2 more times, and finish with the last stitch in the row, 1 SC.

Row 5 completed.

Continue following the chart from rows 6–10. You can check your work row by row to make sure you're on the right track. After row 10, add row 3 again to finish the swatch.

Row 6 completed.

Row 7 completed.

Row 8 completed.

Row 9 completed.

Row 10 completed.

Completed swatch with row 3 added.

Here's what the back of the finished swatch should look like. You can see here that those pockets without any stitches are barely noticeable.

Working in the Round

When working mosaic crochet patterns in the round, you will no longer need to use border stitches, which means no cutting and no tail ends! Each round's color is changed at the back of a seam on one side.

If you've ever used the original "In the Round" tutorial from my website, you'll notice these instructions are a bit different. I've been on a mission to figure out a way to completely hide the seam so the designs are continuous without any visible connecting stitches. Instead of connecting each round with a slip stitch and a chain, all of these rounds are connected from the back side of the project, so the color change between colors A and B are hidden in the back. This technique produces a nearly invisible seam!

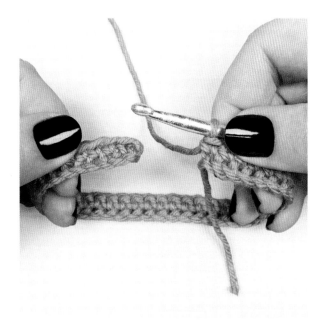 

1. **When working in the round from a foundation row,** begin by crocheting a foundation chain and SC row using the number of stitches indicated for your specific project. Wrap the beginning of the row around to meet the end of the row, making sure all of the stitches are facing out and there are no twists in the row. Connect the bottom of both sides together with a stitch marker or pin to hold the round in place. **If you're crocheting in the round from a circle, skip this step and continue to step 2.**

2. Pull your hook to make the last stitch a wider loop, and take out your hook. Insert your hook from the back to the front, through both loops of the first stitch in the round. **When working in the round from a circle,** insert your hook from the back into both loops of the first SC stitch after the joining chain on the circle.

3. Turn your project so you're looking at the back of the round from the inside. **It's also easier to insert your hook from this angle.** Make sure the working yarn is down toward the inside, and not under your hook on the front side. Insert your hook into the open loop.

4. Tighten the yarn on the hook and slip stitch.

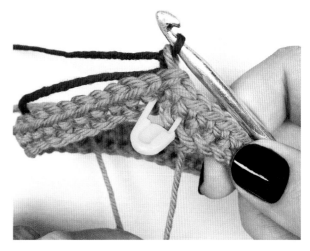

5. Cast on with color B and slip stitch.

6. Tighten color A. **Make sure you don't pull the knot on your hook through the loop.**

    Tighten color B. Chain 1. The first stitch for the next round is directly below your hook.

Working in the Round (continued)

The first stitch for the next round is directly below your hook.

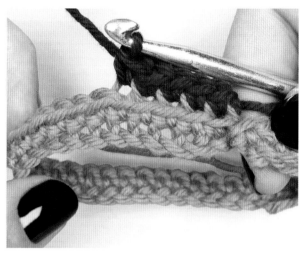

Round 2: SC into the top back loops to the end of the round. **Do not crochet over the tail because you'll need it to close the gap at the bottom of round 1. Only crochet over the tail when you're beginning round 2 from a circle.**

Round 3 and all remaining rounds: Follow steps 2–6 for connecting the round and switching colors.

For a round with no color change, follow steps 2–4, tighten, chain 1 and begin your next round in the stitch below using the same color. To end a round, after the last chain, tighten, cut and pull through.

CLOSING THE GAP

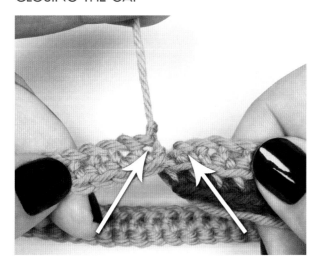

1. To close the gap at the bottom of the foundation chain, turn your project over so the bottom is facing up. You'll be using the tail end from the first chain to weave across both sides and close the gap. **The arrows indicate where you will be inserting your hook on the right and left sides.**

2. Insert your hook from the front to the back on the right side and pull the tail through.

3. Insert your hook from the back to the front on the left side and pull the tail through.

4. Both tail ends will now be on the inside of the round. Tie both tail ends together with a square knot to secure.

Working in the Round (continued)

You can see a very small gap where the seam is, but it's only visible on rounds that start and end with DC stitches.

Inside seam hiding all of the starting chains and color changes.

STITCH PLACEMENT ON A CIRCLE

To crochet in the round from a circle, begin your first round with the number of stitches for your specific pattern.

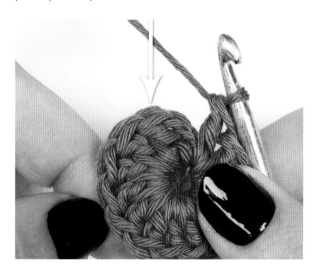 

To join the round, slip stitch into both loops of the first DC in the round after the chain. See the stitch placement in the above photo. Each round will join to the first stitch after the chain.

For the next round, the first stitch will start in the same stitch space as the chain. See the stitch placement in the above photo. Each round will begin in this stitch space.

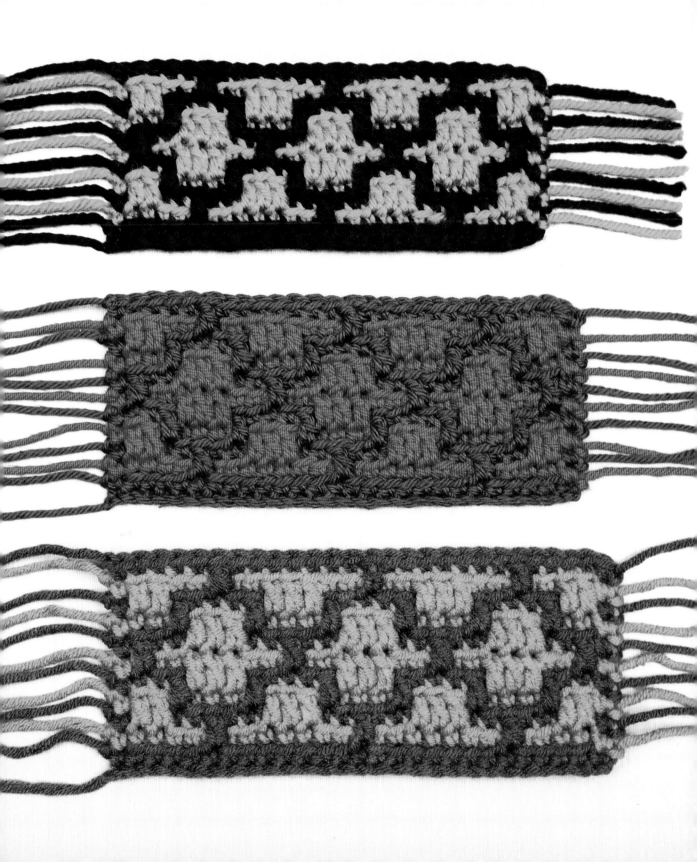

Gauge & Yarn

All of the projects in this book and the swatches on page 23 were crocheted using an H/8 (5 mm) hook and worsted weight yarn.

The most frequent question I get asked is, "Why do my projects come out so much larger than yours?" Sometimes when you're using the same size hook and the same weight yarn, your dimensions will be different because of your tension and the type of yarn you're using. Yarn weight can also vary greatly depending on the fiber content and density, so a project crocheted in worsted acrylic will likely end up being a different size than a project crocheted in worsted wool or cotton. Unfortunately, not all worsted weight yarn is created equal, so you can't always rely on how the label classifies the yarn. Understanding gauge and fiber content will help you crochet projects that are closer to your desired dimensions.

YARN CONTENT

Wool (Teal Swatch)

Projects crocheted in wool tend to come out smaller because the yarn fibers are very stretchy and bounce back when you pull them. Try to choose a smooth wool with the least amount of loose fibers so your mosaic designs come out crisp and clean. Merino wool is my absolute favorite because of its softness and smooth texture, and it also comes in an incredible range of both solids and wild hand-dyed colors.

Cotton (Pink Swatch)

Cotton yarn has no stretch, which makes it great for flat projects. It is much denser than wool so it keeps its shape. Cotton has a clear stitch definition with little to no fuzzy halo around the stitches, making it great for mosaic crochet designs. Projects crocheted in cotton come out larger than wool because the strands are tighter and the lack of stretch produces larger stitches. Pima cotton has longer fibers and is less tightly woven than standard cotton, so it has a better drape and is an excellent choice for wearable items.

Acrylic (Blue Swatch)

Choose a higher quality anti-pilling yarn if you're going to use acrylic. The fibers end up being both dense and bouncy, so there's less stitch definition because the stitches are generally more puffy and take up more space. Projects crocheted in acrylic tend to come out slightly larger than cotton and significantly larger than wool. As far as durability, I wouldn't recommend using acrylic for projects that get a lot of use. Even anti-pilling acrylic tends to have a fuzzy halo and break down over time, which ends up distorting all of the fine details in mosaic crochet designs.

Although all of the projects in this book are crocheted using cotton or wool, you can substitute acrylic yarn for them. You may need to adjust your tension, switch to a smaller hook size or use a lighter weight yarn than what's listed in the pattern in order to stay in the same gauge.

Projects like can cozies, pillows with inserts, plant holders and wearable items are the most important projects to try and stay within the same gauge as the pattern to ensure a proper fit.

GAUGE

Gauge is determined by the number of stitches and rows in 4" (10 cm). You can make a gauge swatch following the tutorial on pages 10–17, using the yarn you'd like to use for your project. Turn your swatch over and use a ruler to count the number of stitches across any of the rows in the middle up to 4" (10 cm). It's less important to count the number of rows you have in 4" (10 cm), because each row is a SC row on the back, and all of the stitches end up measuring close to square.

Check the gauge listed in the pattern and compare it to the number of stitches you have. If you have fewer stitches, you'll need to go down a hook size, crochet tighter, switch to a DK or thinner yarn or all three. If you have more stitches, you'll need to go up a hook size, crochet looser, switch to an Aran weight or thicker yarn or all three.

Ends & Tassels

For flat projects with border stitches, there are a couple of different ways to finish the edges. You can weave all of the border stitches into the back to make a flat edge, or you can incorporate the tail ends into tassels to create fringe. Feel free to have fun with the projects in this book and swap out different fringe options or create flat edges as you see fit.

WEAVING IN THE ENDS

The easiest way to weave in short ends is by weaving in your needle first.

1. From the back, insert your needle through 6 to 8 stitches, after the first border stitch. Line up the eye of the needle so it is just above the border stitch.

2. Thread the needle with the tail end, leaving about a ¼" (6 mm) tail. Pull all the way through.

3. Continue weaving in the ends, matching rows of stitches with the same color tail. If you run out of space weaving in the tails across, you can weave the last tail up through the back of the rows.

Ends & Tassels (continued)

4. Carefully trim the excess tail ends in the back.

Front edge with tail ends woven in the back

ADDING TASSELS AND FRINGE

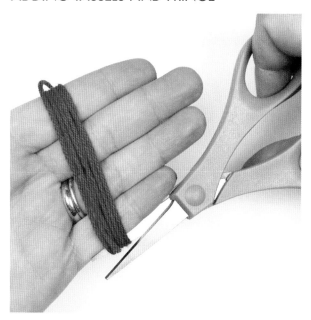

Depending on the pattern, the length of the strands for the tassels can be cut all at once. Measure and cut 1 strand to size, and use that as a guide to see how long you'll need to make the rest of the strands. You can wrap the strands around a piece of cardboard, a deck of cards or even use your hand, then cut 1 side. I find 6" (15.2-cm) tassels are the easiest to cut when you use your hand as a guide. Don't worry about these strands being exactly the right size, because you can trim them all to the correct length while you have them pinned on a blocking mat.

For this example, I'm using 1 of each color strand to match the pattern, folded in half.

1. Begin by inserting your hook under your project, between the first 2 tail end border stitches. Hook your folded strands and pull through a loop.

2. Take the tail ends from the border stitches, 1 on each side of the loop, and add them to the group of tails at the top of the loop.

3. Take all 6 tails and pull them through the loop. Pull the short tails to tighten.

One tassel completed

Ends & Tassels (continued)

For tassels with only 1 color, weave the tail end you don't want to show into the back. Insert your hook next to the border stitch with the tail end and pull through a loop. Add the tail end on the side from the border stitch into the group above the loop. Pull all tails through the loop and pull the short tails to tighten.

For the third tassel, I reversed the colors and wove the gray tail into the back for an all-pink tassel. For the fourth tassel, I wove in both tail ends and used purple for the strands. And finally, the last tassel at the top was made by following the same steps as the first tassel, but with 2 strands per color for a thicker tassel.

Blocking

For flat and straight edges, blocking is key. Mosaics are crocheted from the front side only, and always in the same direction, so this causes your projects to slant on an angle to one side. This may be more visible depending on the type of yarn you're using, but these projects always have a little shift to them. This can be corrected by blocking them on a blocking mat.

Not all projects need to be blocked (I certainly don't block everything I crochet!), but for flat projects like mug rugs, wall hangings and table runners, I highly recommend it. You may also want to block projects that are crocheted in the round, like bags and pillows, because this helps straighten out the seams and makes it easier to line up and attach zippers and other components.

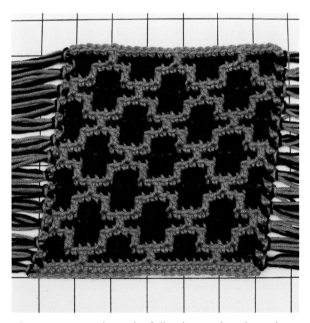

This mug rug is slanted a full 1" (2.5 cm) to the right!

TOOLS
- Water bottle or steamer
- Set of interlocking foam blocking mats
- Stainless steel or rustproof pins

There are two different techniques for blocking: steaming and soaking. I prefer to soak my projects because the water really gets into the stitches and helps move them into place. The projects I've soaked have also stayed straight a lot longer than the projects I've steamed.

Steaming is good for when you only need to straighten out your project a little bit or to help flatten any edges that are curling up. It's also a lot faster because you don't have to wait as long for your project to dry!

SOAKING

Using a spray bottle filled with water (any temperature will work), fully spray the back of your project, making sure you soak the edges and any seams, border stitches and fringe. If you're blocking a bag, turn it inside out and spray the inside first.

Turn it over (or right side out) and fully spray the front of your project, including any tassels or fringe.

PINNING

Position your project on a blocking mat so all 4 corners are aligned on the grid. Pull any corners that are out of alignment and pin them into place, but **do not stretch it out**. If you feel one corner is pulling too tightly, then move it in and move the other side in as well so they're both aligned. If you have one corner that seems loose, that's okay. Pin it into place and push the loose part down with your hand and toward the middle to even it out. **You're trying to finagle your project straight, so don't stretch it out!**

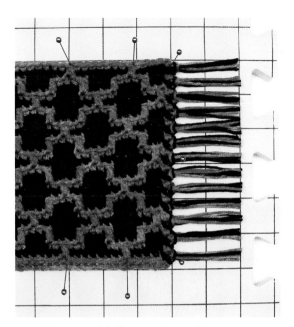

Tassels trimmed following the grid

Continue adding pins along the edges every 1" or 2" (2.5 or 5 cm), aligning it with the grid on the mat. Once you have your project pinned down, you can comb out and straighten any fringe with your fingers and trim it following the lines on the grid.

Allow your project to fully dry before removing the pins. This may take several days depending on humidity.

STEAMING

To steam your project, start with the previous instructions for pinning. Once your project is aligned and pinned to your mat, you can steam it. **If you're using an iron, make sure you're not touching the surface of your project. You don't want to flatten any stitches!** Make sure you're fully steaming the edges and any seams, border stitches and fringe. Allow your project to fully dry before removing any pins.

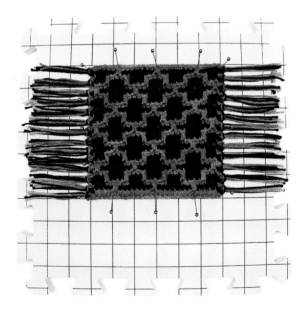

Quick Projects

Let's jump right into some quick projects to warm up your mosaic crochet skills. This chapter starts with some easy projects using basic mosaic crochet stitches and techniques, and introduces some special stitches to create more advanced designs. The patterns in this book are arranged by skill level, so you'll be building your skills as you move through the different projects. The projects in this chapter also make great last-minute gifts and can be made within a few hours or over a weekend.

Tea House Mug Rugs

These quick and easy geometric mug rugs are great for practicing your new mosaic crochet skills! This pattern uses the same chart as the tutorial on pages 9–17, and is expanded to a square size for mugs and drinks. This pattern is worked flat with border stitches, and extra tassels are added to the tail ends to create fringe.

Difficulty· Easy

Supplies for Project
- Standard ruler
- Scissors

Hook
- H/8 (5 mm)

Gauge
- 18 stitches and 18 rows in 4" (10 cm)

Yarn Used
Cascade Nifty Cotton, Worsted, 100% Cotton
- <1 skein (30 yards [27.5 m]) Black
- <1 skein (35 yards [32 m]) Purple, Alexandrite (green), Celestial Blue, Silver

Dimensions
- 6" x 6" (15 x 15 cm), 6" x 10" (15 x 20 cm) with 2" (5-cm) tassels

A Note on Yarn
I recommend only using cotton yarn for this project because it's more absorbent than other yarn fibers. This project also requires very little yarn, so it's perfect for using up cotton scrap yarn.

Tea House Chart

8 stitches in repeat

#	1	2	3	4	5	6	7	8	9	10	11	12	13	14	15	16	17	18	19	20	#
10	X	X							X	X	X								X	X	10
9			X				X							X				X			9
8				X	X	X									X	X	X				8
7	X										X									X	7
6				X	X	X									X	X	X				6
5			X				X							X				X			5
4	X	X							X	X	X								X	X	4
3					X											X					3
2																					2
1																					1

Repeat Section

■ Color A   □ Color B

Stitch Key

	Single Crochet	*All blank boxes SC, top back loop only*
X	**Double Crochet**	*DC in the row below of the same color*

FOUNDATION CHAIN

When calculating your foundation chain, use **multiples of 8 chains plus 1.**

The foundation chain is calculated by the number of repeats across, multiplied by 8, plus 1, plus 2 more for the border stitches.

For a 6" (15-cm) mug rug (3 repeats): 3 x 8 + 1 + 2 = 27

Begin your foundation chain in color A (**outline color**) with 27 chains.

FOLLOWING THE CHART

Your first row is color A (outline color), and your second row is color B (background color), as indicated in the numbered column of the chart.

Row 1: Chain 1 and SC into the second chain from the hook. SC the entire row. Chain 1, pull down to tighten, cut a 3" (7.5-cm) tail and pull through.

Row 2: Start with a border stitch and add SC stitches for the entire row, up to the last stitch. Finish with a border stitch and cut a 3" (7.5-cm) tail. **All remaining rows will start and end with a border stitch.**

Begin following the chart from row 3. Follow across all 8 stitches in the repeat section and repeat those 8 stitches in the repeat section 3 times total. **This chart shows 2 repeats across.** Finish the row with the last stitch in the chart.

Follow the chart from rows 3–10 and begin again from row 3. Add rows 3–10 three times total for a square mug rug. Add row 3 to finish.

Completed mug rug base

ADDING FRINGE

To hide the tail ends and create fringe, cut 5" (12.5-cm) long strands of yarn, 27 strands of each color, or 1 strand for each matching border stitch.

Insert your hook between 2 tail ends under the border stitch. Hook 2 strips of yarn folded in half (1 of each color) and pull through a loop. Add 2 tail ends (one on each side) to the strips and pull all 6 tails through the loop. Pull the short tails to tighten.

Continue adding tassels under every other border stitch (**between 2 tail ends**), and repeat for the other side.

Block your finished mug rug on a blocking mat, and trim yarn fringe to 2" (5 cm) on both sides.

Dripping Can Cozy

Keep your cans cool and your hands dry with this quick and easy dripping can cozy design. This pattern is great for beginners because it uses basic mosaic crochet stitches with the addition of some bobbles for the drippy details. If slime isn't your thing, try using different colors to create dripping coffee, water or even blood! This pattern is worked in the round on a circle base and fits a standard soda can.

Difficulty: Easy

Supplies for Project
- Tapestry needle
- Scissors

Hook
- H/8 (5 mm)

Gauge
- 18 stitches and 18 rows in 4" (10 cm)

Yarn Used (1 Cozy)
Cascade Nifty Cotton, Worsted, 100% Cotton
- <1 skein (53 yards [48.5 m]) Black
- <1 skein (36 yards [33 m]) Lime

Dimensions
- Fits standard soda can 5" x 3" (12.5 x 7.5 cm)

A Note on Yarn
I recommend only using cotton yarn for this project because it's more absorbent than other yarn fibers. This project also uses very little yarn, so it's perfect for using up cotton scrap yarn.

CIRCLE ROUNDS

Start the circle with the yarn color you would like for the bottom of the can. **This will be the background (color A) under the drips.** Chain 4 and slip stitch into the bottom of the first chain to connect. **For all rounds on the circle, work your stitches into both loops.**

Round 1: Chain 2 and add 12 DCs into the center hole, crocheting over the tail.

Note
The first 2 chains for every round do not count as a DC stitch.

To join the round, slip stitch into both loops of the first DC in the round after the chain (see "Stitch Placement on a Circle" [page 22]). **Repeat this step for all remaining rounds on the circle.**

Round 2: Chain 2 and add 2 DCs into the same stitch space as the chain. Add 2 DCs in each stitch to the end of the round. Slip stitch to join. *24 DCs total.*

Round 3: Chain 2 and add 2 DCs into the same stitch space as the chain. Add 1 DC in the next stitch. **Repeat the sequence:** 2 DCs, 1 DC, to the end of the round. Slip stitch to join. *36 DCs total.*

To finish the circle, chain 1 and add 1 round SC stitches into both loops. **This will count as row 1 of the chart.** Continue to "Following the Chart" below.

Dripping Chart

12 stitches across

#	1	2	3	4	5	6	7	8	9	10	11	12	#
18	X	X	X	X	X	X	X	X	X	X	X	X	18
17													17
16	X		X	X	X	X	X		X	X	X	X	16
15		X					X						15
14	X		X	X	X	X	X		B	X	X		14
13		X					X	X				X	13
12	X		X		X	X	B			X	X		12
11		X		X			X	X	X			X	11
10	X		B		X	X				X	B		10
9		X	X	X			X	X	X		X	X	9
8	B					B	X				X		8
7	X	X		X	X		X	X	X		X	X	7
6			X			X				B			6
5	X	X		X	X		X	X	X	X	X	X	5
4			B			X							4
3	X	X	X	X	X		X	X	X	X	X	X	3
2							B						2
1													1

 Color A   Color B

Can Size

To ensure a proper fit, place your can on the circle. The circle should be a little wider than the base of the can. If it's not the correct size, you may need to use a different yarn or hook (see "Gauge & Yarn" [page 24]).

Stitch Key

For step-by-step instructions of special stitches, please refer to the pages listed below.

	Single Crochet	*All blank boxes SC, top back loop only*	
X	Double Crochet	*DC in the row below of the same color*	
B	Bobble	*2 DCs decreased together in the same stitch*	*Page 164*

FOLLOWING THE CHART

Your first round is color A (**background**), and second round color B (**drip color**), as indicated in the numbered column of the chart.

Follow steps 2–6 for "Working in the Round" (pages 18–19) to join round 1, and cast on with color B to start round 2.

All remaining rounds will follow the "Working in the Round" instructions (page 18) for joining and switching colors.

The bobble stitches in the chart are not overlay stitches, so you will begin following the chart from row 2. Follow across all 12 stitches in the row and repeat these 12 stitches 3 times total to the end.

Follow the chart from rows 2–18. To finish the top of the edge, add 1 round of slip stitches into both loops using color B.

To end after the join, chain 1, tighten, cut about a 4" (10-cm) tail and pull through. Weave the tail end on the inside at the seam so it is next to the yarn from the last color change. Cut the other color and leave about a 4" (10-cm) tail end. Tie both tail ends together with a square knot. Weave in all ends on the inside.

STITCHES ON BOBBLES

When adding a SC stitch on top of a bobble, be sure to hook the very back loop of the bobble, behind the top loop.

SC stitch in the back loop behind the bobble.

When adding a DC stitch to a bobble, hook the front loop.

DC stitch in the front loop of the bobble.

Heartbreaker Zipper Pouch

Create a cute broken heart zipper pouch that's great for holding makeup, crochet hooks, pens—or you can even use it as a clutch for going out! This design is crocheted in the round, with a zipper hand-sewn on the top and the bottom stitched closed from the inside.

Difficulty Intermediate

Supplies for Project
- 7" (18-cm) closed-end zipper
- Needle and thread
- Tapestry needle
- Scissors

Hook
- H/8 (5 mm)

Gauge
- 18 stitches and 18 rows in 4" (10 cm)

Yarn Used
- Purple & Black
  Cascade Nifty Cotton, Worsted, 100% Cotton
  - <1 skein (90 yards [82.5 m]) Grape (purple)
  - <1 skein (70 yards [64 m]) Black

- Black & Silver
  Cascade Nifty Cotton, Worsted, 100% Cotton
  - <1 skein (90 yards [82.5 m]) Black
  Ice Yarns, Rock Star, Worsted, Polyamide Blend
  - <1 skein (70 yards [64 m]) Silver

Dimensions
- 8" x 5.5" (20 x 14 cm)

A Note on Yarn
This project uses very little yarn, so it's perfect for using up scrap yarn or for experimenting with different textures like metallic yarn.

Heartbreaker Chart

11 stitches in repeat

#													#
13	X	X	X			X	X	X		X	X	X	13
12		D̄	D	D	D̄		D̄	D	D	D̄			12
11	X	X				⟍				X	X		11
10		X	X	X		X	X	X	X	X			10
9	X	D	D̄				⟍	D̄	D	X			9
8			X	X	X		X	X	X				8
7	X	X	D	D̄		⟍		D̄	D	X	X		7
6				X		X	X	X					6
5	X	X	X	D	D̄	⟍		D̄	D	X	X	X	5
4				X		X							4
3	X	X	X	X	D	D̄		D̄	D	X	X	X	3
2													2
1													1

Repeat Section

Color A Color B

Stitch Key

For step-by-step instructions of special stitches, please refer to the pages listed below.

	Single Crochet	All blank boxes SC, top back loop only	
X	Double Crochet	DC in the row below of the same color	
D̄D	DC Dec End SC	2 DCs decreased, SC above 2nd DC	Page 171
DD̄	DC Dec Start SC	SC, 2 DCs decreased below	Page 170
＼」	Diagonal Up	SC, DC below, skip	Page 166
∟／	Diagonal Down	Skip, DC, SC above	Page 167

FOUNDATION CHAIN

When calculating your foundation chain, use **multiples of 11 chains plus 2.**

To calculate your foundation chain, start with the number of hearts you would like across, multiplied by 11, plus 2. Double this stitch count for the back of the bag.

For a pouch with 3 hearts across: (3 x 11 + 2) x 2 = 70

Begin your foundation chain in color A (**background color**) with 70 chains, or the appropriate stitch count for your specific size.

FOUNDATION ROUNDS

Your first round is color A (background), and your second round is color B (heart color), as indicated in the numbered column of the chart.

Round 1: Chain 1 and SC into the second chain from the hook. SC to the end.

Follow the instructions for "Working in the Round" (page 18) to join round 1, switch colors, and add round 2 of the chart. All remaining rounds will follow the "Working in the Round" instructions for joining and switching colors.

FOLLOWING THE CHART

Begin following the chart from row 3. Start with the first stitch in the row before the repeat section. Follow across all 11 stitches in the repeat section and repeat those 11 stitches 3 times total, or to your desired size. Finish side 1 with the last stitch in the row after the repeat section. For side 2, repeat these steps again.

Follow the chart from rows 3–13, and begin again from row 2. Add rows 2–13 for a second section of hearts. Finish with 1 round of slip stitches into the top back loops with color A.

Slip stitch from the back to join. Chain 1, tighten, cut about a 4" (10-cm) tail and pull through. Weave the tail end on the inside at the seam so it is next to the yarn from the last color change. Cut the other color and leave about a 4" (10-cm) tail end. Tie both tail ends together with a square knot. Weave in all ends on the inside.

MAKING THE ZIPPER POUCH

Before closing the bottom and adding a zipper, block the finished pouch on a blocking mat, making sure the seam is straight and the other side of the fold is also even on both sides.

To close the bottom, turn the pouch inside out and position it so the foundation chain is at the top. Using color A, secure your yarn at the seam through the first stitch on both sides with a knot. Insert your hook through the first stitch, pull through a loop and add slip stitches through both the front and back panels to the end. To finish, chain 1, tighten, cut, pull through and weave in the tail ends. Turn the bag right side out.

1. To add a zipper, align a closed zipper with the tape just under the crocheted panel, with the pull side positioned at the seam. Double thread a needle with thread matching the color of the base, and begin adding back stitches from the inside through the zipper at the seam, under the round of slip stitches of the crocheted panel.

2. Continue all the way to the end of the zipper and stitch across the end.

3. To continue to the back, open the zipper, align the tape under the crocheted panel and continue adding back stitches to the end.

4. Angle the tape ends down toward the inside and stitch them in place so they don't poke out of the top of the pouch.

Zipper attached

REFERENCE PHOTOS

The following reference photos are an example of some of the more complex rows in the chart. These serve as a visual guide so you can check your progress and make sure you're on the right track.

Row 3

Row 5

Row 7

Row 12

Wrought Iron Headbands & Belts

This versatile scroll pattern can be made into many different lengths to create headbands, hatbands, high-waisted belts and hip belts. This pattern is worked flat with border stitches and the tail ends are used as cords to tie the band together with a bow or knot, so there are no ends to weave in! You can even add embellishments like beads or tie the cords to a metal loop for some extra flair. This project also uses very little yarn, so you can even make these using scrap yarn.

Difficulty: Intermediate to Advanced

Supplies for Project
- 18" (45-cm) ruler
- Scissors
- Optional Embellishments: wide hole beads, metal ring

Hook
- H/8 (5 mm)

Gauge
- 19 stitches in 4" (10 cm)

Yarn Used
Malabrigo Rios, Worsted, 100% Merino Wool
- <1 skein Sunset (orange), Holly Hock (pink), Gris (gray), Indiecita (green-blue)

Berroco Modern Cotton, Worsted, Pima Cotton & Modal Blend
- <1 skein Longspur (black)

Dimensions
- 4 Scroll Headband—16" (40.5 cm), 44" (112 cm) total with cords, 36 yards (33 m) orange, 18 yards (16.5 m) black
- 5 Scroll Hatband—20" (51 cm), 48" (122 cm) total with cords, 48 yards (44 m) pink, 24 yards (22 m) black
- 9 Scroll Gray Belt—36" (91 cm), 64" (162.5 cm) total with cords, 66 yards (60.5 m) gray, 42 yards (38.5 m) black
- 11 Scroll Green-Blue Belt—44" (112 cm), 72" (183 cm) total with cords, 78 yards (71.5 m) green-blue, 54 yards (49.5 m) black

Each scroll section measures about 4" (10 cm), plus 14" (35.5-cm) cords on each side.

For a custom size, measure your desired length in inches and divide by 4 (**divide by 10 when measuring in cm**). Round to the nearest whole number. This will be the total number of scroll sections across. Subtract 2 scrolls to accommodate for stretch and enough space to tie the cords together. Use this number of scrolls when calculating your foundation chain for a custom size.

A Note on Yarn
This pattern uses a combination of wool and a cotton blend, but you can also create this design using all cotton, all wool or even scrap yarn. I chose this yarn combination for the beautiful semi-variegated colors in the wool, and because the cotton gives these bands structure.

Wrought Iron Chart

36 stitches in repeat, or 18 stitches per scroll

Chart (read right to left / left to right, rows numbered 1–9 on each side):

Row																																				Row
9	X	X					X	X	X	X	2	/					X	X					\	2	X	X	X	X					X	X		9
8																																				8
7	X		2	/		X		X	2	/	D̄	D			X	X			X	X			D	D̄	\	2	X		X		\	2		X	X	7
6		X											X	X																		X				6
5	X		X	X			2	/	D̄	D	X		X		D̄	D		D	D̄		X		X	D	D̄	\	2			X	X		X		5
4																																				4
3	X	X					D̄	D	X	X	X			X	X					X	X	X	X	D	D̄					X	X				3
2																																				2
1																																				1

Repeat Section

Color A ☐   Color B ▨

Stitch Key

For step-by-step instructions of special stitches, please refer to the pages listed below.

Symbol	Name	Description	Page
	Single Crochet	All blank boxes SC, top back loop only	
X	**Double Crochet**	DC in the row below of the same color	
D̄ D	**DC Dec End SC**	2 DCs decreased, SC above 2nd DC	*Page 171*
D D̄	**DC Dec Start SC**	SC, 2 DCs decreased below	*Page 170*
2 /	**2 DCs**	Skip, 2 DCs in next stitch	*Page 165*
\ 2	**2 DCs**	2 DCs, skip the next stitch	*Page 165*
\	**Diagonal Up**	SC, DC below, skip the next stitch	*Page 166*
/	**Diagonal Down**	Skip the next stitch, DC, SC above	*Page 167*

FOUNDATION CHAIN

When calculating your foundation chain, use **multiples of 18 chains plus 2**.

To calculate your foundation chain, start with the number of scrolls you would like across, multiplied by 18, plus 2, plus 2 more for the border stitches.

For a headband with 4 scrolls: 4 x 18 + 2 + 2 = 76

For a hatband with 5 scrolls: 5 x 18 + 2 + 2 = 94

Custom size: *Number of scrolls* x 18 + 2 + 2

Begin your foundation chain with the appropriate stitch count above for your specific length. **Measure an 18" (45-cm) tail before casting on. Each row will begin and end with an 18" (45-cm) tail.**

FOLLOWING THE CHART

Your first row is color A (background), and your second row is color B (scroll color), as indicated in the numbered column of the chart.

Row 1: Chain 1 and SC into the second chain from the hook. SC the entire row. Chain 1, pull down to tighten, cut an 18" (45-cm) tail and pull through.

Row 2: Start with a border stitch and add SC stitches for the entire row, up to the last stitch. Finish with a border stitch and cut an 18" (45-cm) tail. **All remaining rows will start and end with a border stitch and an 18" (45-cm) tail on both sides.**

Begin following the chart from row 3. Start with the first stitch in the row before the repeat section. Follow across all 36 stitches in the repeat section (both scroll sections) and repeat these 36 stitches in the repeat section again to your desired size. **For an odd number of scrolls across, you will end the row after the 18 stitches in the first scroll section.** Finish the row with the last stitch in the row after the repeat section.

Follow the chart from rows 3–9. To finish the top of the band, add 1 row of slip stitches (loosely) into the top back loops using color A.

MAKING CORDS

These cords are made by twisting the tail ends together in 4 separate groups. The left side of the band will have 11 tail ends, and the right side will only have 9. For an even number on both sides, you'll need to add 2 more tails to the very first border stitch on the bottom right.

1. Cut a 36" (91-cm) length of color A yarn, and fold it in half. Insert your hook under the first border stitch on the bottom right side of the band.

2. Pull through a loop, and pull the 2 tails through the loop. Tighten.

3. Secure the band to a solid base with a clip, or use something heavy like a book to hold it in place. Divide the tails into 2 groups—5 tails on one side and 6 tails on the other. At the base of the band, tie a knot with each group of tails.

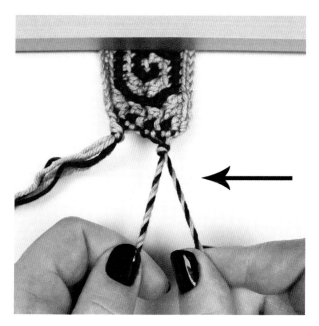 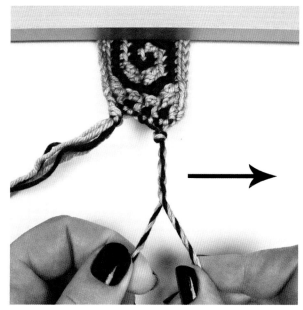

4. Starting with one group, split the tails again—2 on one side and 3 on the other—or 3 and 3. Working in small sections, begin twisting both tail groups separately to the left.

5. Twist both groups over each other to the right. Continue twisting separately to the left, and together to the right until you have 3" to 4" (7.5 to 10 cm) of tails remaining.

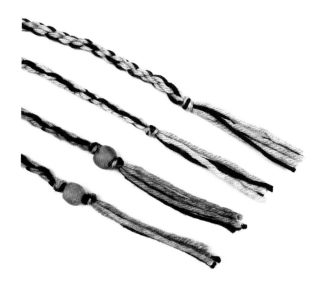

6. Tie a knot at the end of the twists to secure. To add a bead, leave about 6" (15 cm) of tails before tying a knot. String your bead over all of the tails, and add another knot to the bottom of the bead to secure it. Repeat for all 4 tail sections. Trim any uneven tails.

7. Block your finished band on a blocking mat.

The following reference photos are an example of some of the more complex rows in the chart. These serve as a visual guide so you can check your progress and make sure you're on the right track. These are broken down into right and left scrolls in reference to the chart.

Row 4 - Right

Row 4 - Left

Row 5 - Right

Row 5 - Left

Row 6 - Right

Row 6 - Left

Row 7 - Right

Row 7 - Left

Row 8 - Right

Row 8 - Left

Wearable Accessories

Are you ready to cover yourself in mosaic crochet? With the right type of yarn, you can create wearable mosaic crochet accessories that are edgy, eye-catching and comfortable. All these projects are customizable to fit your specific measurements or can be made larger or smaller by changing the number of repeats in the pattern. You can even make some of these projects small enough for children, so the whole family can be covered in mosaic crochet!

The projects in this chapter are arranged by skill level from easy to advanced, so you can strengthen your skills as you accessorize your wardrobe.

Fishnet Scarf

Fishnets that will actually keep you warm! This sexy little design is perfect for beginners that are learning special stitches, and with a very short repeat it's easy to get into the groove and follow the flow of the pattern. This design works well with bold contrasting colors, but you could also go classic with black and a neutral flesh-tone background color. This pattern is worked flat with border stitches, and extra tassels are added to the tail ends to create fringe.

Difficulty: Easy

Supplies for Project
- Standard ruler
- Scissors

Hook
- H/8 (5 mm)

Gauge
- 19 stitches and 19 rows in 4" (10 cm)

Yarn Used

Misfit Yarns, Superwash Merino Worsted, 100% Merino Wool
- 1 skein (218 yards [200 m]) Pink Punk

Cascade Yarns, 220 Superwash Merino Worsted, 100% Merino Wool
- 1 skein (220 yards [201 m]) Black

Dimensions
- 6' (183-cm) scarf: 72" x 4" (183 x 10 cm) (78" [198 cm] long with tassels)
- 5' (152.4-cm) scarf: 60" x 4" (152 x 10 cm) (66" [167.6 cm] long with tassels)

Fishnet Chart

6 stitches in repeat

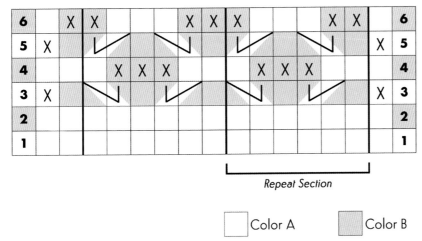

Repeat Section

Color A   Color B

Stitch Key

For step-by-step instructions of special stitches, please refer to the pages listed below.

	Single Crochet	All blank boxes SC, top back loop only	
X	Double Crochet	DC in the row below of the same color	
 ∨	Diagonal Down	Skip the next stitch, DC, SC above	Page 167
 ╲╷	Diagonal Up	SC, DC below, skip the next stitch	Page 166

FOUNDATION CHAIN

When calculating your foundation chain, use **multiples of 6 chains plus 3.**

The foundation chain is calculated by the number of repeats across, multiplied by 6, plus 3, plus 2 more for the border stitches.

For a 6' (183-cm) scarf (56 repeats): 56 x 6 + 3 + 2 = 341

For a 5' (152.4-cm) scarf (47 repeats): 47 x 6 + 3 + 2 = 287

Begin your foundation chain in color A (**fishnet color**), with the appropriate stitch count above for your specific size.

FOLLOWING THE CHART

Your first row is color A (fishnet color), and your second row is color B (background color), as indicated in the numbered column of the chart.

Row 1: Chain 1 and SC into the second chain from the hook. SC the entire row. Chain 1, pull down to tighten, cut a 3" (7.5-cm) tail and pull through.

Row 2: Start with a border stitch and add SC stitches for the entire row, up to the last stitch. Finish with a border stitch and cut a 3" (7.5-cm) tail. **All remaining rows will start and end with a border stitch.**

Begin following the chart from row 3. Start with the first stitch in the row before the repeat section. Follow across all 6 stitches in the repeat section and repeat those 6 stitches in the repeat section again to your desired size. **The chart shows 2 repeats.** Finish the row with the last 2 stitches in the row after the repeat section.

Follow the chart from rows 3–6. Repeat rows 3–6 as many times as you like to make your scarf wider, and finish with row 3 or 5. For a 4" (10-cm)-wide scarf (as shown in the example) add rows 3–6, 4 times and finish with row 3.

ADDING FRINGE

To hide the tail ends and create fringe, cut 6" (15-cm)-long strands of color A and color B.

Insert your hook between 2 tail ends under the border stitch. Hook 2 strips of yarn folded in half (1 of each color) and pull through a loop. Add 2 tail ends (1 on each side) to the strips and pull all 6 tails through the loop. Pull the short tails to tighten.

Continue adding tassels under every other border stitch (between 2 tail ends) and repeat for the other side.

Block your finished scarf on a blocking mat and trim any excess yarn fringe so it is even on both ends.

REFERENCE PHOTOS

The following reference photos are an example of some of the more complex rows in the chart. These serve as a visual guide so you can check your progress and make sure you're on the right track.

Row 3

Row 5

In Chains Messenger Bag

This simple chain link design is flipped on its side to create an edgy yet functional cross-body messenger bag. You can easily add a pop of color or go wild and make every chain a different color! This bag is a great size for carrying books, tablets and crochet projects, and you can customize the strap to make three different lengths. This pattern is worked flat with border stitches and is assembled sideways so the tail ends will be at the bottom and the top.

Difficulty : Easy to Intermediate

Supplies for Project
- Standard ruler
- Soft tape measure
- Scissors
- Tapestry needle
- Stitch markers

Hook
- H/8 (5 mm)

Gauge
- 18 stitches and 18 rows in 4" (10 cm)

Yarn Used
Cascade Nifty Cotton, Worsted, 100% Cotton
- 3 skeins (550 yards [503 m]) Black
- 1.5 skeins (265 yards [242.5 m]) Silver

Misfit Yarns Superwash Merino Worsted, 100% Merino Wool
- <1 skein (45 yards [41 m]) Lemon

Bag Dimensions
- 13" x 10" x 2" (33 x 20 x 5 cm) fully assembled

A Note on Yarn
If you'd like to make your chain link sections different colors, you'll need about 45 yards (41 m) of each color, or about 310 yards (283.5 m) total for all color B rows. You can use cotton, wool or acrylic for the chain link sections, as long as the thickness of the yarn is similar to the cotton yarn used for color A.

In Chains — Large Links Chart

9 stitches in repeat

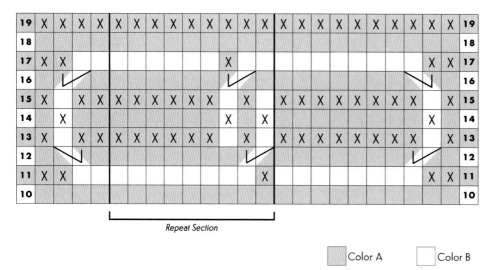

Repeat Section

Color A   Color B

In Chains — Small Links Chart

6 stitches in repeat

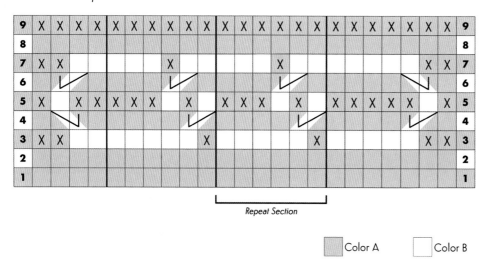

Repeat Section

Color A   Color B

Stitch Key

For step-by-step instructions of special stitches, please refer to the pages listed below.

	Single Crochet	*All blank boxes SC, top back loop only*	
X	**Double Crochet**	*DC in the row below of the same color*	
 ∠	**Diagonal Down**	*Skip the next stitch, DC, SC above*	*Page 167*
 ∖	**Diagonal Up**	*SC, DC below, skip the next stitch*	*Page 166*

FOUNDATION CHAIN

The height of the bag base is a fixed size, 16 large links tall. There are 2 large links for every 3 small links.

Begin your foundation chain in color A (**background color**) with 151 chains.

This stitch count includes the 2 border stitches for the beginning and end of the row.

FOLLOWING THE CHARTS

Your first row is color A (background), and your second row is color B (link color), as indicated in the numbered column of the charts.

Row 1: Chain 1 and SC into the second chain from the hook. SC the entire row. Chain 1, pull down to tighten, cut a 3" (7.5-cm) tail and pull through.

Row 2: Start with a border stitch and add SC stitches for the entire row, up to the last stitch. Finish with a border stitch and cut a 3" (7.5-cm) tail. **All remaining rows will start and end with a border stitch.**

Chain Link Section 1

Begin following the Small Links Chart from row 3. Start with the first 7 stitches in the row before the repeat section. Follow across all 6 stitches in the repeat section and repeat those 6 stitches again, 23 times total. **This chart shows 2 repeats across.** Finish the row with the last 4 stitches in the chart. Follow the Small Links Chart from rows 3–9.

Chain Link Section 2

Begin following the Large Links Chart from row 10. Start with the first 10 stitches in the row before the repeat section. Follow across all 9 stitches in the repeat section and repeat those 9 stitches again, 15 times total. Finish the row with the last 4 stitches in the chart. Follow the Large Links Chart from rows 10–19.

Chain Link Sections 3 & 4

Follow both charts again, from rows 2–19.

Chain Link Sections 5 & 6

Add rows 2–19 again, and switch to yellow yarn for rows 10–18 (**color B rows only**). **Row 18 will be entirely hidden under a row of all DC stitches, so this row can be yellow or gray.**

Chain Link Section 7

Add rows 2–7.

If you want to change the color of other chain link sections, switch colors on rows 2–8 for small links and 10–18 for large links (color B rows only).

REFERENCE PHOTOS

The following reference photos are an example of some of the more complex rows in the chart. These serve as a visual guide so you can check your progress and make sure you're on the right track.

Row 4 - Left

Row 6 - Right

Chain Link Sections 1 and 2.

ADDING FRINGE

Weave all of the tail ends on the left side of the panel into the back. This will become the top edge of the inside opening of the bag. The tail ends on the right side will become the fringe for the bottom edge of the bag's front flap.

Measure and cut 7" (18-cm) strips of yarn: 30 black, 25 gray, 5 yellow (or 30 color A, 30 color B).

To add fringe to the right side, insert your hook between the first border stitch with 1 tail end on each side. Hook 2 strips of yarn folded in half (1 of each color matching the colors of the tail ends) and pull through a loop. Add 2 tail ends (1 on each side) to the strips and pull all 6 tails through the loop. Pull the short tails to tighten.

Continue adding tassels between every other border stitch (between 2 tail ends) to the end.

Block your finished bag base on a blocking mat and trim any excess yarn fringe so it is even.

MAKING A STRAP

- 53" (134.5-cm) strap: 319 chains
- 50" (127-cm) strap: 307 chains
- 47" (120-cm) strap: 295 chains

To figure out your strap size, use a soft tape measure across your body from your front right hip, over your left shoulder and to the back of your right hip. Keep in mind the bag will stretch and hang below your hip—if you want it to be shorter, use the measurements for the next size down. Begin your foundation chain with the appropriate stitch count above with the measurements closest to your strap length. **These stitch counts include the 2 border stitches for the beginning and end of the row.**

The total length of the strap will be about 20" (51 cm) longer than the measurements on page 69; 10" (25.5 cm) on each side will be attached to the base of the bag.

Follow the instructions for the Small Links Chart, rows 1–7.

Weave the tail ends on both sides into the back.

Finish the strap with a border: After row 7, start with a border stitch and add 1 row of SC stitches into both loops to the end of the row. Chain 1 and add slip stitches under all the border stitches to the end. Add slip stitches across the bottom row **loosely**, to the end. Add slip stitches between all the border stitches to the end. Chain 1, tighten, cut, pull through and weave both tails into the back of the strap.

ATTACHING THE STRAP

Use 4 stitch markers to mark the 45th stitch from the bottom of both sides of the strap.

Lay the bag base right side down, with the fringe at the top. Fold the bottom up about two-thirds of the way. Position the strap so the stitch markers line up with the top of the opening.

You will be attaching the strap with SC stitches into **both loops** of the bag base and strap.

Insert your hook into the first stitch on the top left of the base (**top right if crocheting left-handed**) and under the first stitch marked on the strap. Using color A, pull a tail through and tie a knot to secure the yarn to the base and strap. Insert your hook back into the hole. Pull through a loop and chain 1.

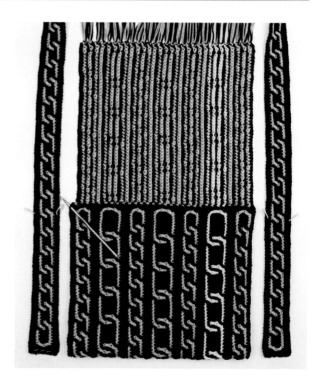

Working over the tail, add SC stitches through the base and the strap to the end of the strap.

Corner: At the end of the strap, insert your hook into the next stitch on the base and back into the last stitch on the strap, SC. Repeat again with the next stitch on the base and back into the same hole on the strap, SC. There will be 3 SC in the same stitch of the bottom corner of the strap and 3 consecutive SCs on the base.

Bottom of strap: Add SC stitches into the holes **above** the border stitches to cover them (7 stitches across).

Corner: Insert your hook into the next stitch on the base and into the first stitch on the back of the strap, SC. Insert your hook into the next stitch on the base and back into the same hole on the strap, SC. Repeat again. There will be 3 SC in the same stitch of the bottom corner of the strap and 3 consecutive SCs on the base.

Continue connecting the strap to the base with SCs in the outside loops of the strap, 45 stitches across, stopping in the marked stitch.

Bottom of strap attached to bag base.

Do not add any more stitches to the strap. Add slip stitches across the edge of the bag base to the end.

Continue adding slip stitches across the bottom, into the holes under each of the border stitches. **These are not the same holes as the fringe, but just below them (62 stitches across).**

Mark the 50th stitch across from the bottom (**fringe side**) with a stitch marker, and continue adding slip stitches (**49 stitches across**) up to the stitch marker.

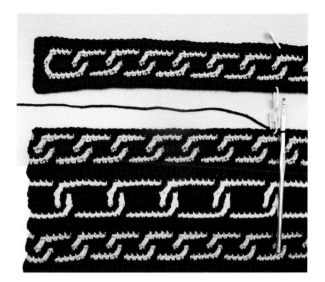

Align the other side of the strap to the base so both stitch markers line up. **Make sure the strap is flat and there are no twists.**

Insert your hook into the marked stitch on the base and under the marked stitch on the strap, SC. Continue connecting the base and strap with SCs to the end.

Repeat the steps for the corners and the bottom of the strap. Continue connecting the base and strap with SCs to the end of the base and into the last marked stitch on the strap. Chain 1, tighten, cut, pull through and weave tail into inside of bag.

Poison Skull Cap

Cute little toxic skulls and crossbones circle the edge of this skull cap beanie hat. This pattern is worked from the top down and crocheted in the round from a circle base. The mosaic skull section is worked upside down. This hat can be made in three different sizes and can be made either form-fitted or oversized and slouchy.

Difficulty: Intermediate

Supplies for Project
- Soft tape measure
- Tapestry needle
- Scissors

Hook
- H/8 (5 mm)

Gauge
- Circle Rounds: 17 stitches and 10 DC rows in 4" (10 cm)
- Mosaic Section: 18 stitches and 18 rows in 4" (10 cm)

Hat Measurements
Measure around the head from the middle of the forehead to the bottom of the head just above the neck. Note the measurement to the nearest inch or cm. Use the sizes listed below to find how many skulls you'll need for the pattern.

- **Kids/Small:** Up to 19" (48.5 cm)—*6 skulls around*
- **Adult Medium:** 19" to 22" (48.5 to 56 cm)—*7 skulls around*
- **Adult Large:** 22" to 25" (56 to 63.5 cm)—*8 skulls around*

A Note on Yarn: This pattern is an opportunity to use wild variegated yarns, but be sure to choose a solid color for the skulls.

A Note on Fit
For a more accurate fit, I recommend crocheting a row of SC stitches to use as a size guide. This way you can use whatever yarn you like and not have to worry about staying in the same gauge as the pattern! Chain 104 and add a row of SC stitches. Use this to measure around your head. Each skull is 13 stitches wide. The full length of the guide will be 8 skulls, 13 stitches less will be 7 skulls, and 26 stitches less will be 6 skulls.

Yarn Used for Adult Large Size
- Pink and White Hat
  Threads by Megan Nicole, Superwash Merino Worsted, 100% Merino
    - *1 skein (100 yards [91.5 m]) Nevermore*
  Paintbox Wool Mix Aran, Wool/Acrylic Blend
    - *<1 skein (40 yards [36.5 m]) White*

- Variegated Orange and Black Hat
  Threads by Megan Nicole, Superwash Merino Worsted, 100% Merino
    - *1 skein (80 yards [73 m]) Starburst*
  Paintbox Wool Mix Aran, Wool/Acrylic Blend
    - *<1 skein (60 yards [55 m]) Black*

CIRCLE ROUNDS

Start the circle with the yarn color you would like for the base of your hat. **This will be the background (color A) for the skull section.** Chain 4 and slip stitch into the bottom of the first chain to connect.

For all rounds on the circle, work your stitches into both loops.

Round 1: Chain 2 and add 13 DCs into the center hole, crocheting over the tail.

> Note
> **The first 2 chains for every round do not count as a DC stitch.**

To join the round, slip stitch into both loops of the first DC in the round after the chain (see "Stitch Placement on a Circle" [page 22]). **Repeat this step for all remaining rounds on the circle.**

Round 2: Chain 2 and add 2 DCs into the same stitch space as the chain. Add 2 DCs in each stitch to the end of the round. Slip stitch to join. *26 DCs total.*

Round 3: Chain 2 and add 2 DCs into the same stitch space as the chain. Add 1 DC in the next stitch. Repeat the sequence: 2 DCs, 1 DC, to the end of the round. Slip stitch to join. *39 DCs total.*

Round 4: Chain 2 and add 2 DCs into the same stitch space as the chain. Add 1 DC in the next 2 stitches. Repeat the sequence: 2 DCs, 1 DC, 1 DC, to the end of the round. Slip stitch to join. *52 DCs total.*

Round 5: Chain 2 and add 1 DC into the same stitch space as the chain. Add 1 DC in each stitch to the end. Slip stitch to join. *52 DCs total.*

Round 6: Chain 2 and add 2 DCs into the same stitch space as the chain. Add 1 DC in the next 3 stitches. Repeat the sequence: 2 DCs, 1 DC, 1 DC, 1 DC, to the end of the round. Slip stitch to join. *65 DCs total.*

Round 7: Chain 2 and add 1 DC into the same stitch space as the chain. Add 1 DC in each stitch to the end. Slip stitch to join. *65 DCs total.*

Round 8: Chain 2 and add 2 DCs into the same stitch space as the chain. Add 1 DC in the next 4 stitches. Repeat the sequence: 2 DCs, 1 DC, 1 DC, 1 DC, 1 DC, to the end of the round. Slip stitch to join. *78 DCs total.*

Round 9: Chain 2 and add 1 DC into the same stitch space as the chain. Add 1 DC in each stitch to the end. Slip stitch to join. *78 DCs total.*

For a Kids/Small hat with 6 skulls around, stop here and join from the back, following the "Working in the Round" steps 2–6 on pages 18–19. **This last round will count as row 1 of the Poison Chart.**

Round 10: Chain 2 and add 2 DCs into the same stitch space as the chain. Add 1 DC in the next 5 stitches. Repeat the sequence: 2 DCs, 1 DC, 1 DC, 1 DC, 1 DC, 1 DC, to the end of the round. Slip stitch to join. *91 DCs total.*

Round 11: Chain 2 and add 1 DC into the same stitch space as the chain. Add 1 DC in each stitch to the end. Slip stitch to join. *91 DCs total.*

For an Adult Medium hat with 7 skulls around, stop here and join from the back following the "Working in the Round" steps 2–6 on pages 18–19. **This last round will count as row 1 of the Poison Chart.**

Round 12: Chain 2 and add 2 DCs into the same stitch space as the chain. Add 1 DC in the next 6 stitches. Repeat the sequence: 2 DCs, 1 DC, 1 DC, 1 DC, 1 DC, 1 DC, 1 DC, to the end of the round. Slip stitch to join. *104 DCs total.*

Round 13: Chain 2 and add 1 DC into the same stitch space as the chain. Add 1 DC in each stitch to the end. Slip stitch to join. *104 DCs total.*

For an Adult Large hat with 8 skulls around, stop here and join from the back following the "Working in the Round" steps 2–6 on pages 18–19. **This last round will count as row 1 of the Poison Chart.**

Poison Chart

13 stitches across

13	X	X	\	2	X	X	X	X	X	2	/	X	X	13
12			X								X			12
11	X		\	2				2	/			X		11
10			\	⌟	X	X	X	⌎	/					10
9	X	X	X	X						X	X	X	X	9
8			X		X		X							8
7	X	X	2	/		B		B		\	2	X	X	7
6			⌎	/	X	X	X	X	X	\	⌟			6
5	X				D	D̄				D̄	D		X	5
4			X								X			4
3	X	X	D̄	D	X	X	X	X	X	D	D̄	X	X	3
2														2
1														1

☐ Color A   ▨ Color B

Stitch Key

For step-by-step instructions of special stitches, please refer to the pages listed below.

Symbol	Stitch	Description	Page
	Single Crochet	*All blank boxes SC, top back loop only*	
X	Double Crochet	*DC in the row below of the same color*	
D D̄	DC Dec Start SC	*SC, 2 DCs decreased below*	*Page 170*
D̄ D	DC Dec End SC	*2 DCs decreased, SC above 2nd DC*	*Page 171*
＼⌟	Diagonal Up	*SC, DC below, skip the next stitch*	*Page 166*
⌎／	Diagonal Down	*Skip the next stitch, DC, SC above*	*Page 167*
＼2	2 DCs	*2 DCs, skip the next stitch*	*Page 165*
2／	2 DCs	*Skip, 2 DCs in next stitch*	*Page 165*
B	Bobble	*2 DCs decreased together in the same stitch*	*Page 164*

FOLLOWING THE CHART

Your first round is color A (background), and your second round is color B (skull color), as indicated in the numbered column of the chart.

After completing the circle rounds for your desired size, join the last round from the back, following the instructions for "Working in the Round" steps 2–6 (pages 18–19). Continue following the instructions to add round 2. All remaining rounds will follow the "In the Round" instructions for joining and switching colors.

Begin following the chart from row 3. Follow across all 13 stitches in the row and repeat these 13 stitches again to fit your size (6 times for Kids/Small, 7 times for Adult Medium, 8 times for Adult Large).

Follow the chart from rows 3–13.

FINISHING THE EDGE

To finish the outer edge you can join and switch to color B for a stripe at the bottom or use color A for the remaining rounds.

All remaining rounds will be crocheted into both loops and joined from the back.

Chain 2, add 1 round of DC stitches, join. Chain 1 and add 1 round of SC stitches, join. **You can continue adding alternating rounds of DCs and SCs to create a wider edge.**

To end after the join, chain 1, tighten, cut about a 4" (10-cm) tail and pull through. Weave the tail end on the inside at the seam so it is next to the yarn from the last color change. Cut the other color and leave about a 4" (10-cm) tail end. Tie both tail ends together with a square knot. Weave in all ends on the inside.

When adding SC stitches on top of the bobbles on row 8, be sure to hook the very back loop of the bobble, behind the top loop.

REFERENCE PHOTOS

The following reference photos are an example of some of the more complex rows in the chart. These serve as a visual guide so you can check your progress and make sure you're on the right track.

Row 5

Row 6

Row 7

Row 10

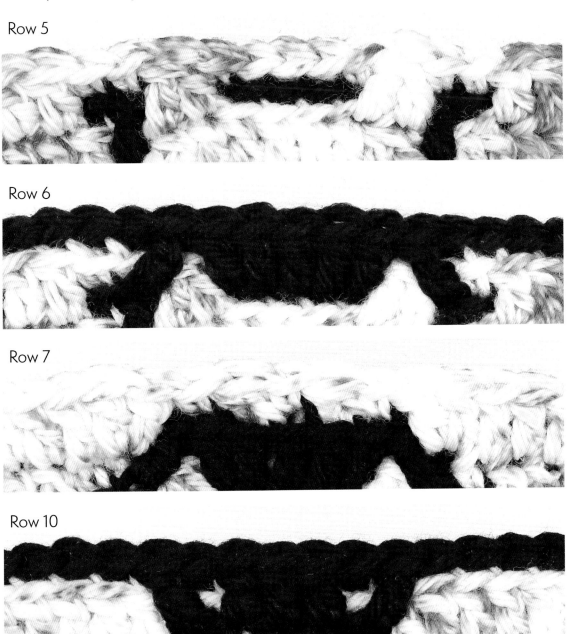

Spine Arm Warmers

Create some long, spiky spines for your arms for when you want that sci-fi meets archeology look! This pattern is worked in the round and split with border stitches to create thumbholes. You can fully customize these arm warmers to fit your measurements. These can be made shorter for quick fingerless gloves or crocheted all the way up to your elbows for some serious drama.

Difficulty: Intermediate

Supplies for Project

- Stitch markers
- Soft tape measure
- Tapestry needle
- Scissors

Hook

- H/8 (5 mm)

Gauge

- 19 stitches and 19 rows in 4" (10 cm)

Custom Fit Measurements

- **Width Around:** Using a soft measuring tape, measure loosely around the palm of your hand, just under your fingers. Note the measurement to the nearest inch or cm.
- **Thumbhole:** Measure from under the second knuckle on your pointer finger to just before the webbing on your thumb. From that point, measure to the base of your thumb for the opening. Make a note of both measurements.

Yarn Used

- Purple Arm Warmers (9" long x 8" around [23 x 20 cm])
  Cascade 220 Superwash Merino, Worsted, 100% Merino
  - *1 skein (150 yards [137 m]) Violet Heather (purple)*
  - *1 skein (120 yards [110]) Flint Gray (light gray)*

- Black Arm Warmers (12" long x 8" around [30.5 x 20 cm])
  Cascade 220 Superwash Merino, Worsted, 100% Merino
  - *1 skein (220 yards [201 m]) Black*
  - *1 skein (140 yards [128 m]) December Sky (dark gray)*

A Note on Yarn

For best results, use two solid contrasting colors for this design. The fine line details can sometimes get lost when using semi-solid or variegated yarns. Go for bold!

Spine Chart

13 stitches across each spine

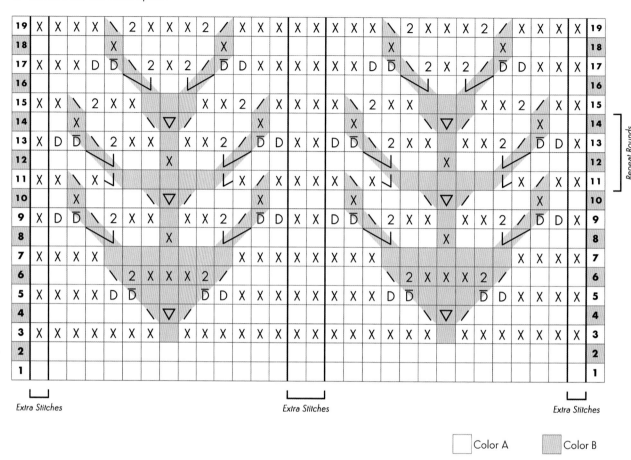

Repeat Rounds

☐ Color A ▨ Color B

Extra Stitches

Stitch Key

For step-by-step instructions of special stitches, please refer to the pages listed below.

	Single Crochet	*All blank boxes SC, top back loop only*	
X	**Double Crochet**	*DC in the row below of the same color*	
\ ▽ /	**Triangle**	*Skip, DC, SC above, DC below in same stitch, skip*	*Page 176*
D̄ D	**DC Dec End SC**	*2 DCs decreased, SC above 2nd DC*	*Page 171*
D D̄	**DC Dec Start SC**	*SC, 2 DCs decreased below*	*Page 170*
2 /	**2 DCs**	*Skip, 2 DCs in next stitch*	*Page 165*
\ 2	**2 DCs**	*2 DCs, skip the next stitch*	*Page 165*
└	**Diagonal Down**	*Skip the next stitch, DC, SC above*	*Page 167*
╲	**Diagonal Up**	*SC, DC below, skip the next stitch*	*Page 166*
└X/	**Double Diagonal Down**	*Skip the next stitch, DC, DC, SC above*	*Page 169*
\X⌐	**Double Diagonal Up**	*SC, DC below, DC, skip the next stitch*	*Page 168*

FOUNDATION CHAIN

Each arm warmer will have one spine on the front and one on the back, with extra stitches added in between to expand the size. The extra stitches marked in the chart are where you will add these extra duplicate stitches (**beginning, middle and end of chart**) based on the stitch counts on the right. The extra stitches on the seam side are split between the beginning and end of the round, so when you're following the chart you're starting with the first half of extra stitches and finishing the round with the other half.

Using the measurements for the width around your palm (see "Custom Fit Measurements" [page 81]), find the appropriate stitch count listed below:

- 6" (15 cm)—no extra stitches (full chart) = **30 chains total**
- 7" (18 cm)—add 4 extra stitches to the chart (split 1, 2, 1) = **34 chains total**
- 8" (20 cm)—add 8 extra stitches to the chart (split 2, 4, 2) = **38 chains total**
- 9" (23 cm)—add 12 extra stitches to the chart (split 3, 6, 3) = **42 chains total**

For larger sizes, add extra stitches in multiples of 4, split 1, 2, 1.

Begin your foundation chain in color A (**background color**), with the appropriate stitch count for your specific size.

FOUNDATION ROUNDS

Your first round is color A (background), and your second round is color B (spine color), as indicated in the numbered column of the chart.

Round 1: Chain 1 and SC into the second chain from the hook. SC to the end.

Follow the instructions for "Working in the Round" (page 18) to join round 1, switch colors and add round 2 of the chart. All remaining rounds will follow the "Working in the Round" instructions for joining and switching colors.

MARKING YOUR EXTRA STITCHES

The best way to set up your stitches for round 3 is by marking your extra stitches with stitch markers first. Starting at the seam, count the extra stitches you'll need for the beginning of the round and mark that last stitch. Leave a 13-stitch space for the first spine section. Count and mark the first and last stitch of the extra stitches you'll need for the middle. Leave a 13-stitch space for the second spine section. Mark the next stitch. The remaining stitches to the seam will be the extra stitches to the end of the round. **Once you have round 3 established with stitch markers, you can easily add the same number of extra stitches for the next round, and the spine sections in the chart will be much easier to follow!**

FOLLOWING THE CHART

Begin following the chart from row 3. Start with the first extra stitch in the row and any added stitches. Follow across all 13 stitches in the first spine section. Add the next 2 stitches in the middle of the chart and any added stitches. Follow across all 13 stitches in the second spine section. Add the last extra stitch in the row and any added stitches.

Follow the chart from rows 3–14, **but stop before you've reached the height of your first thumbhole measurement (at about round 10). For your next round, you will be adding border stitches and creating a thumbhole.**

THUMBHOLES

Begin your next round as usual. At the end of the round, insert your hook into both stitches of the last stitch and add a border stitch. Cut the yarn and leave a tail. **Make a note of which round you're starting and ending the thumbhole so your second arm warmer will have the thumbhole in the same spot.**

Border stitch in the last stitch of the round.

Begin your next round with a border stitch into both loops of the first stitch of the last round and finish the round with a border stitch on top of the border stitch from the previous row. **Your extra stitches on the seam side will decrease by 2 because you're now using those stitches as border stitches.**

Border stitch on top of border stitch.

To reduce the number of tail ends you'll need to weave in for the thumbholes, you can crochet over the beginning and end tails of color A with color B rows.

Next round with both beginning and ending border stitches.

Continue following the chart, repeating rows 11–14 (**Repeat Rounds**).

When you've reached the height for the opening for your thumbholes, you will stop adding border stitches and continue crocheting in the round again. At the end of your next color A row, add 1 SC into the top back loop of the last border stitch. Pull up a loop, remove your hook and insert your hook through the back of both loops of the first border stitch on the next row. Pull through the loop to connect, chain 1, tighten. Cast on color B, tighten color A and chain 1. **All remaining rows will be worked in the round.**

Round connected.

Stitches in the round over border stitches.

Continue repeating rows 11–14 to your desired size.

If at any point you need to increase the width of the arm warmer to fit your forearms, you can add 2 extra DC stitches to any color A rows in the middle of the chart. The next color B round will have 2 extra SC stitches in the middle. **Adding extra stitches to the middle section only will help keep the spine design centered up the arm instead of veering over to the outside of the arm.**

To finish, add rows 15–19, and add 1 round of SC stitches into both loops with color A.

To end after the join, chain 1, tighten, cut about a 4" (10-cm) tail and pull through. Weave the tail end on the inside at the seam so it is next to the yarn from the last color change. Cut the other color and leave about a 4" (10-cm) tail end. Tie both tail ends together with a square knot. Weave in the ends on the inside.

FINISHING THE EDGES

Bottom edge border.

Position the arm warmer so the first round is at the top. Insert your hook into the first stitch at the seam and cast on with color A. Add slip stitches loosely across the bottom chain to the end of the round. Connect from the back (as you would crocheting in the round), chain 1, tighten, cut and pull through.

Turn the arm warmer inside out and weave in any tails.

To finish the edge of the thumbhole, insert your hook into both loops of the stitch at the bottom of the opening and cast on with color B. Add slip stitches under each border stitch, across the stitches at the seam and between the border stitches on the other side. Continue adding slip stitches to the end. Connect from the back into the first stitch (as you would crocheting in the round) chain 1, tighten, cut and pull through.

Repeat all steps to create a second arm warmer.

Thumbhole border.

Finished thumbhole.

REFERENCE PHOTOS

The following reference photos are an example of some of the more complex rows in the chart. These serve as a visual guide so you can check your progress and make sure you're on the right track.

Row 9

Row 10

Row 11

Row 12

Row 17

Stellar Shawl

Make a bold, dramatic statement with this eye-catching five-pointed star pattern. This shawl is crocheted upside down, from the wide end to the bottom point, and is decreased by two stitches in each row to create a classic triangle shape. This pattern is worked flat with border stitches and has tassels made from the tail ends. All of the other tail ends are worked into the next row, so there are very few ends to weave in!

 Advanced

Supplies for Project
- Standard ruler
- Scissors
- Tapestry needle

Hook
- H/8 (5 mm)

Gauge
- 19 stitches and 19 rows in 4" (10 cm)

Yarn Used
Berroco Pima 100, Worsted, 100% Pima Cotton
- 5 skeins (910 yards [832 m]) Black Eyed Susan (black)
- 3 skeins (600 yards [548.6 m]) Chrysanthemum (gold)

Dimensions
- 60" x 30" (152.5 x 76 cm) (not including tassels)

A Note on Yarn
I highly recommend using a light worsted or DK weight yarn for this project. A medium worsted or thicker weight yarn will end up producing a much larger and heavier shawl than the dimensions listed. For more information on gauge and sizing, see page 24.

FOUNDATION CHAIN
When calculating your foundation chain, use **multiples of 24 chains plus 43.**

To calculate your foundation chain, start with one less than the number of stars you would like across the top (**for 11 stars, use 10**), multiplied by 24, plus 43, plus 2 more for the border stitches.

For a shawl with 11 stars across the top: 10 x 24 + 43 + 2 = 285

Begin your foundation chain in color A (**background color**) with 285 chains, or the appropriate stitch count for your specific size.

Stellar Left Corner Chart

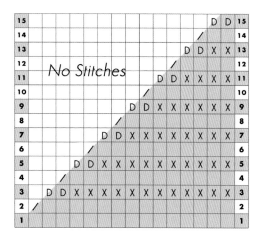

Stellar Right Corner Chart

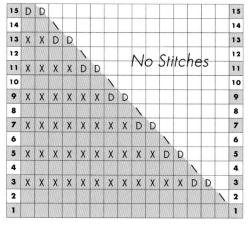

Color A   Color B

Stitch Key

/ \	Skips	Skip the next stitch
D D	DC Decrease	2 DCs decreased (no SC added)

Stellar Center Chart

24 stitches in repeat

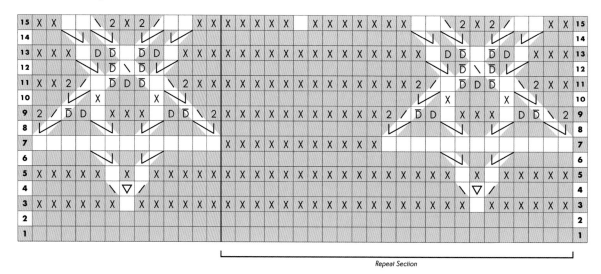

Repeat Section

Color A   Color B

Stitch Key

For step-by-step instructions of special stitches, please refer to the pages listed below.

	Single Crochet	All blank boxes SC, top back loop only	
X	Double Crochet	DC in the row below of the same color	
\ ▽ /	Triangle	Skip, DC, SC above, DC below in same stitch, skip	Page 176
∨	Diagonal Down	Skip the next stitch, DC, SC above	Page 167
∖	Diagonal Up	SC, DC below, skip the next stitch	Page 166
\ 2	2 DCs	2 DCs, skip the next stitch	Page 165
2 /	2 DCs	Skip, 2 DCs in next stitch	Page 165
D D̄	DC Dec Start SC	SC, 2 DCs decreased below	Page 170
D̄ D	DC Dec End SC	2 DCs decreased, SC above 2nd DC	Page 171
D̄ D D̄	DC Dec 3 Together	SC, 3 DCs decreased below, SC above 3rd DC	Page 173
D̄ \ D̄	DC Dec Centered	SC, start decrease below, skip, finish decrease, SC above	Page 174

FOLLOWING THE CHARTS

Your first row is color A (background), and your second row is color B (star color), as indicated in the numbered column of the charts.

Row 1: Chain 1 and SC into the second chain from the hook. SC the entire row. Chain 1, pull down to tighten, cut a 3" (7.5-cm) tail and pull through.

Row 2: Start with a border stitch, **skip the next stitch** and add SC stitches for the entire row, until you have 2 stitches left. **Skip the second to last stitch.** Finish with a border stitch and cut a 3" (7.5-cm) tail. **All remaining rows will start and end with a border stitch on top of the previous row's border stitch.**

Each row will start with the Stellar Right Corner Chart, then continue to the Stellar Center Chart and finish with the Stellar Left Corner Chart. Each row will decrease by 2 stitches, one on each side.

Begin following the Stellar Right Corner Chart from row 3, all stitches shaded in purple across the row. Continue to the Stellar Center Chart from row 3. Follow across all 24 stitches in the repeat section and repeat those 24 stitches in the repeat section again to your desired size (**10 repeats for a shawl with 11 stars**). Finish the row with the last 13 stitches in the row after the repeat section (**the 11th star**). Continue to the Stellar Left Corner Chart from row 3, all stitches shaded in purple across the row.

All color B tail ends will be made into tassels and all color A tail ends will be crocheted over with SC stitches or woven into the back.

Begin following the charts for row 4 and start by crocheting over the tail from the previous row. Stop about 2" (5 cm) before the end of the row (or before you start adding SC stitches) and pull the tail back over the row to crochet over it to the end. Repeat this process for all color B rows. **There are enough SC stitches in the corner sections to lock in these color A tail ends so you don't have to weave them all in later.**

Start crocheting over the end tail at about 2" (5 cm) to the end of the row. If the tail end is a little loose, you can gently tighten it by pulling the tail in the back.

When you're beginning a row with a decrease, make sure you're crocheting on top of the first DC stitch and not the top of the decrease stitch from the previous row. The decrease is the stitch you're skipping over. The image to the left shows where to start the decrease, over the DC.

Follow all 3 charts from rows 4–15, and begin again from row 4. Continue adding rows 4–15 until you have only 2 stars left on your shawl. **Each star section will decrease by 1 star.**

Continue to the Stellar Last Star Chart (on the right).

Stellar Last Star Chart

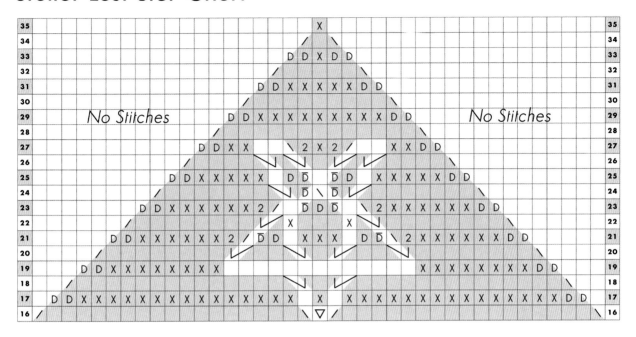

 Color A   Color B

Follow the Stellar Last Star Chart from rows 16–28. On row 29, after adding the ending border stitch, measure about 2 yards (1.8 m) of extra yarn, cut and pull all the way through. Pull the long tail back over to the beginning of the row and begin row 30 by crocheting over this long tail.

You will continue using the same strand of color A yarn by pulling the tail back over the row for rows 31, 33 and 35. Finish the chart with rows 31–35. Weave any extra color A tail ends into the back.

TASSELS AND BORDER

To create tassels, cut 6" (15-cm)-long strands of yarn, 1 for each color B border stitch.

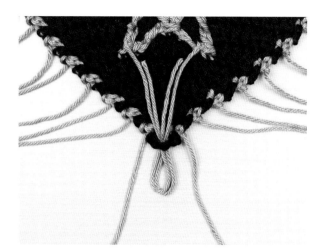

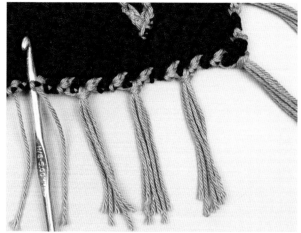

Starting from the bottom point, add 2 strands of yarn, folded in half into both loops of the last DC stitch at the center. Combine the 2 tail ends from the right and left side of the stitch into the group, pull all 6 strands through the loop and pull the short tails to tighten.

Working along the right side of the shawl, in between the next pair of two tail ends, add 2 strands of yarn folded in half and combine the 2 tail ends on the sides into the group. Pull all 6 strands through the loop and tighten. Repeat for the left side of the shawl, starting from the bottom point.

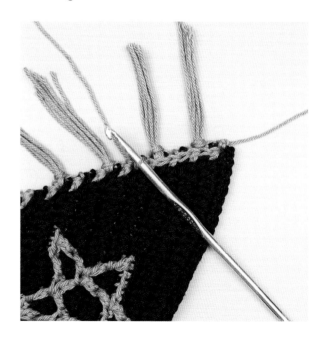

To add a finishing border along the sides, position your shawl so the point is at the top. Using color B for the border, insert your hook into the first border stitch on the bottom right and pull through a strand. Fasten with a knot to connect the yarn to the top edge of the shawl. Insert your hook back into the first border stitch and pull through a loop. Begin adding slip stitches loosely between each of the border stitches on the right side, through the center point at the end and under each border stitch on the left side to the end. **If your slip stitches are too tight, it will cause the shawl to curve in at the edges.**

To finish, chain 1, tighten, cut and pull through. Weave the beginning and end tails into the back.

Block the finished shawl on a blocking mat and trim any uneven tassels. Trim any excess yarn in the back from woven-in tail ends.

REFERENCE PHOTOS

The following reference photos are an example of some of the more complex rows in the chart. These serve as a visual guide so you can check your progress and make sure you're on the right track.

Row 4

Row 8

Row 9

Row 10

Row 11

Row 12

Row 13

Row 14

Star completed.

Home Décor

Just ask my mother and she'll tell you: you can never have too many pillows! Mosaic crochet is excellent for creating pillows and home décor, because the overlay stitches produce a solid woven fabric that works great for objects that need structure and get a lot of use. And what's not to love about adding lots of color, texture and small works of art to your home?

The projects in this chapter are also arranged by skill level from intermediate to advanced, so by the time you get through the final projects, you can call yourself a mosaic crochet pro!

Sanctuary Wall Hanging

Create your own sanctuary with some bold color therapy for your walls. This quatrefoil/ clover design was inspired by old gothic architecture and stained glass windows and is a great pattern for using colorful, hand-dyed yarn. This pattern is worked flat with border stitches and is hung sideways so the tail ends will be at the bottom and the top.

Difficulty : Intermediate

Supplies for Project
- Standard ruler
- Scissors
- Tapestry needle
- Wooden dowel, painted to match background color—12" (30 cm) for banner or 18" (45 cm) for wall hanging
- Optional embellishments: wide-hole beads or crystals

Hook
- H/8 (5 mm)

Gauge
- 18 stitches and 18 rows in 4" (10 cm)

Yarn Used
- Long Purple Banner—6 x 3 clovers
  Cascade Nifty Cotton, Worsted, 100% Cotton
    - *2 skeins (325 yards [297 m]) Black*
  Sweet Georgia Superwash Worsted, 100% Merino Wool
    - *1 skein (200 yards [183 m]) Magician*

- Large Teal Wall Hanging—7 x 5 clovers
  Cascade Nifty Cotton, Worsted, 100% Cotton
    - *3 skeins (400 yards [366 m]) Black*
  Tangled Pixie, Aran, 100% Merino Wool
    - *2 skeins (350 yards [320 m]) Atlantis*

Dimensions
- Long Banner: 10.5" x 21" (27 x 53.5 cm) (10.5" x 26" [27 x 66 cm] with tassels)
- Large Wall Hanging: 17" x 25" (43 x 63.5 cm) (17" x 30" [43 x 76 cm] with tassels)

A Note on Yarn
This pattern uses a combination of wool and cotton, but you can also make this design in all cotton. I chose this yarn combination for the beautiful variegated colors in the wool, and the cotton will lay flatter against a wall than wool or acrylic. Cotton is also less likely to curl up in the corners, and the addition of tassels and beads will help weigh it down and let it lay even flatter. When using 2 skeins of variegated yarn, alternate between skeins for each color B row.

Sanctuary Chart

16 stitches in repeat

Repeat Rows

Repeat Section

Color A

Color B

Stitch Key

For step-by-step instructions of special stitches, please refer to the pages listed below.

	Single Crochet	*All blank boxes SC, top back loop only*	
X	**Double Crochet**	*DC in the row below of the same color*	
D̄ D	**DC Dec End SC**	*2 DCs decreased, SC above 2nd DC*	*Page 171*
D D̄	**DC Dec Start SC**	*SC, 2 DCs decreased below*	*Page 170*
2 /	**2 DCs**	*Skip, 2 DCs in next stitch*	*Page 165*
\ 2	**2 DCs**	*2 DCs, skip the next stitch*	*Page 165*
\ X ⌐	**Double Diagonal Up**	*SC, DC below, DC, skip the next stitch*	*Page 168*
∟ X /	**Double Diagonal Down**	*Skip the next stitch, DC, DC, SC above*	*Page 169*

FOUNDATION CHAIN

When calculating your foundation chain, use **multiples of 16 chains plus 1.**

To calculate your foundation chain, start with the number of clovers you would like for the height, multiplied by 16, plus 1, plus 2 more for the border stitches.

For a long banner with 6 clovers: 6 x 16 + 1 + 2 = 99

For a large wall hanging with 7 clovers: 7 x 16 + 1 + 2 = 115

Begin your foundation chain in color A (**background color**) with the appropriate stitch count above for your specific size.

FOLLOWING THE CHART

Your first row is color A (background), and your second row is color B (clover color), as indicated in the numbered column of the chart.

For longer tassels at the bottom of the banner, start each color A row (after row 1) with a 6" (15-cm) tail before beginning a border stitch. For left-handed crocheters, finish all color A rows with a 6" (15-cm) tail. All other tail ends will be woven in, so you can keep those at around 3" (7.5 cm) long.

Row 1: Chain 1 and SC into the second chain from the hook. SC the entire row. Chain 1, pull down to tighten, cut a 3" (7.5-cm) tail and pull through.

Row 2: Start with a border stitch and add SC stitches for the entire row, up to the last stitch. Finish with a border stitch and cut a 3" (7.5-cm) tail. **All remaining rows will start and end with a border stitch and all remaining color A rows will start with a 6" (15-cm) tail.**

Begin following the chart from row 3. Start with the first 8 stitches in the row before the repeat section. Follow across all 16 stitches in the repeat section and repeat those 16 stitches in the repeat section again to your desired size. Finish the row with the last 9 stitches in the row after the repeat section.

Follow the chart from rows 3–23. For a banner with 3 clover sections up (**2 in between**), start the chart over from row 8 and continue to row 23. Finish with rows 24–31. For a large wall hanging with 5 clover sections up (**4 in between**), repeat rows 8–23 three more times. Finish with rows 24–31.

ATTACHING THE DOWEL

Begin by weaving in all of the tail ends on the left side. This will become the top of the wall hanging where you will attach the dowel. **You can also fold these tail ends down in the back if you don't want to weave them all in, but I would recommend at least weaving in the tails 2" to 3" (5 to 7.5 cm) in on the sides so they don't end up poking out the sides and becoming visible from the front.**

On the right side, weave in all color B tails. This will become the bottom of the wall hanging and you will use the long color A tails as tassels.

Position your wall hanging so the long tail ends are at the top and the flat edge with the tail ends woven in is at the bottom. Insert your hook into the first border stitch on the top right (top left when crocheting left-handed) and cast on with color A. Begin adding slip stitches in between each of the border stitches across the row and into both loops of the last border stitch.

Chain 1 and add SC stitches into both loops across the side to the end.

You will now attach the dowel at the top while adding slip stitches into the border stitches.

Loosely wrap the yarn over the back of the dowel to the front and slip stitch under the first border stitch. Continue adding slip stitches across the row, loosely wrapping the dowel before each stitch. **If you've wrapped the dowel tightly and need to recenter it, you can twist the dowel back and forth while pushing the wrapped stitches over a little at a time.**

To finish the other side, continue adding slip stitches loosely into both loops across the row to the end. Pull the last loop a little bit and take your hook out. Insert your hook through the back of the very first border stitch and pull the loop through to the back. Chain 1, tighten, cut a tail and pull through. Tie both tail ends together with a square knot and weave the tails into the back.

To add a crochet chain at the top for hanging the banner, start with a 6" (15-cm)-long tail and chain 50. Cut a 6" (15-cm)-long tail, pull through the last stitch and tighten. To attach to the dowel, wrap the tail around the dowel twice and tie it to the chain with the knot facing the back. Weave in the tail to the back and repeat for the other side of the dowel.

For a wall hanging larger than the banner, I would recommend making the chain with 2 strands of yarn so it can support the weight. You can also attach it directly to the wall by hanging the dowel across 2 angled nails.

ADDING BEADS AND TASSELS

Separate the tail ends at the bottom into groups of 4. The large wall hanging will have 1 less tail end (1 group of 3).

Thread your yarn (color A) onto a tapestry needle and insert the needle from the back to the front between the first and second tails and under the row of slip stitches. Thread your bead or crystal (optional).

Insert your needle from the front to the back between the third and fourth tails, under the row of slip stitches. Pull the yarn so the bead is hanging loosely below the edge of the banner. **If you're not adding a bead, pull the yarn taut so it is straight across the base of the banner. You can also add extra strands of yarn in between to make the tassels fuller.**

Cut the yarn so it is the same length as the other tails. Tie all 6 tail ends together with a knot close to the bottom of the banner.

Block your finished wall hanging on a blocking mat and trim any uneven tassels.

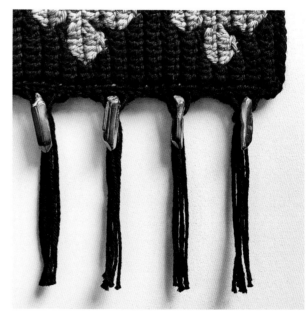

REFERENCE PHOTOS

The following reference photos are an example of some of the more complex rows in the chart. These serve as a visual guide so you can check your progress and make sure you're on the right track.

Row 4

Row 6

Row 7

Row 8

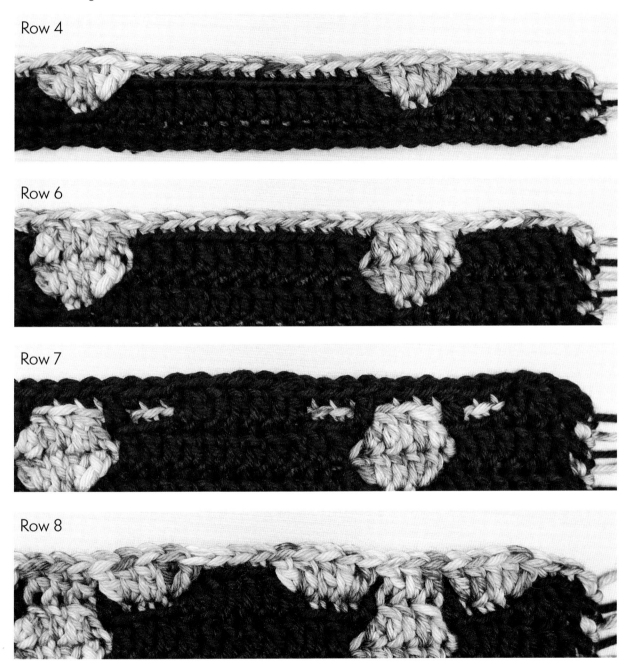

Row 10

Row 11

Row 12

Row 14

Skulls & Stripes Bolster Pillow

Create a bold accent piece with this striped bolster pillow covered in classic skulls. This pattern is worked in the round and vertically, with the skulls crocheted sideways to eliminate any tail ends. The bolster is assembled with two crocheted circles and attached with a contrasting edge.

Difficulty: Intermediate

Supplies for Project

- Tapestry needle
- Scissors
- 6" x 18" (15 x 45-cm) bolster pillow foam insert, roll of batting or fiberfill

Hook

- H/8 (5 mm)

Gauge

- 19 stitches and 19 rows in 4" (10 cm)

Yarn Used

Berroco Ultra Wool, Worsted, 100% Wool

- 2 skeins (290 yards [265 m]) Cast Iron (black)
- 2 skeins (290 yards [265 m]) Snow (white)
- Plus 75 yards (68.5 m) for 2 circles

Dimensions

- Fits a 6" x 18" (15 x 45-cm) bolster pillow insert

Skulls & Stripes Chart

15 stitches across

#	1	2	3	4	5	6	7	8	9	10	11	12	13	14	15	#
22	X	X	2	/		L					X	X	X	X		22
21		D̄	D	X	X	L		\	2							21
20	2	/				X	2	/						X		20
19		X	X	X	X	X	D	D̄	L			X	X	X		19
18	X														X	18
17		X	X	X	X	X	2	/			X	X	X			17
16	D	D̄				X	X	X							X	16
15			\	2	X	X	L		D̄	D						15
14	X	X	D	D̄						X	X	X	X			14
13																13
12																12
11	X	X	2	/		L					X	X	X	X		11
10		D̄	D	X	X	L		\	2							10
9	2	/				X	2	/						X		9
8		X	X	X	X	X	D	D̄	L			X	X	X		8
7	X														X	7
6		X	X	X	X	X	2	/			X	X	X			6
5	D	D̄				X	X	X							X	5
4			\	2	X	X	L		D̄	D						4
3	X	X	D	D̄						X	X	X	X			3
2																2
1																1

Color A   Color B

Stitch Key

For step-by-step instructions of special stitches, please refer to the pages listed below.

	Single Crochet	*All blank boxes SC, top back loop only*	
X	**Double Crochet**	*DC in the row below of the same color*	
⟍⟍	**Diagonal Up**	*SC, DC below, skip the next stitch*	*Page 166*
∠	**Diagonal Down**	*Skip the next stitch, DC, SC above*	*Page 167*
D̄ D	**DC Dec End SC**	*2 DCs decreased, SC above 2nd DC*	*Page 171*
D D̄	**DC Dec Start SC**	*SC, 2 DCs decreased below*	*Page 170*
⟍ 2	**2 DCs**	*2 DCs, skip the next stitch*	*Page 165*
2 ╱	**2 DCs**	*Skip, 2 DCs in next stitch*	*Page 165*

FOUNDATION CHAIN

When calculating your foundation chain, use **multiples of 15 chains**.

The foundation chain is calculated by the number of skulls around, multiplied by 15.

For a bolster pillow with 6 skulls around (6" [15-cm]-wide diameter): 6 x 15 = 90

Begin your foundation chain in color A (**background color**) with 90 chains.

FOUNDATION ROUNDS

Your first round is color A (background of the first skull section), and second round color B (skull color in the first section), as indicated in the numbered column of the chart.

Round 1: Chain 1 and SC into the second chain from the hook. SC to the end.

Follow the instructions for "Working in the Round" (page 18) to join round 1, switch colors and add round 2 of the chart. All remaining rounds will follow the "Working in the Round" instructions for joining and switching colors.

A Note on Fit

If you're planning on stuffing your bolster with a foam tube, try the first round on the tube to see whether it fits. If it's not the correct size, you may need to make a new round using a different yarn or hook (see "Gauge & Yarn" [page 24] and "Dimensions" [page 113]).

FOLLOWING THE CHART

Begin following the chart from row 3. Follow across all 15 stitches in the row and repeat these 15 stitches 6 times to the end of the round.

Follow the chart from rows 3–22, and begin again from row 1. You can add rows 1–22 as many times as you like to make your bolster pillow longer. For an 18" (45-cm) length as shown in the example, add rows 1–22 four times total. Finish with 1 round of SC stitches in both loops with the same color as your last round.

To end after the join, chain 1, tighten, cut about a 4" (10-cm) tail and pull through. Weave the tail end on the inside at the seam so it is next to the yarn from the last color change. Cut the other color and leave about a 4" (10-cm) tail end. Tie both tail ends together with a square knot.

Block your finished tube flat on a blocking mat to straighten the seam and remove any twists.

CIRCLE ROUNDS

Start the circle with the yarn color you would like for the side of your bolster pillow.

In the example, the left side of the pillow has a black background and a black circle connected with white, and the right side has a white background with a white circle connected with black. **You can match the circles to the background colors at the ends, reverse them or make them both the same color. Get creative!**

Chain 4 and slip stitch into the bottom of the first chain to connect.

For all rounds on the circle, work your stitches into both loops.

Round 1: Chain 2 and add 13 DCs into the center hole, crocheting over the tail.

> Note
> **The first 2 chains for every round do not count as a DC stitch.**

To join the round, slip stitch into both loops of the first DC in the round after the chain. (See "Stitch Placement on a Circle" [page 22].) **Repeat this step for all remaining rounds on the circle.**

Round 2: Chain 2 and add 2 DCs into the same stitch space as the chain.

Add 2 DCs in each stitch to the end of the round. Slip stitch to join. *26 DCs total.*

Round 3: Chain 2 and add 2 DCs into the same stitch space as the chain. Add 1 DC in the next stitch. Repeat the sequence: 2 DCs, 1 DC, to the end of the round. Slip stitch to join. *39 DCs total.*

Round 4: Chain 2 and add 2 DCs into the same stitch space as the chain. Add 1 DC in the next 2 stitches. Repeat the sequence: 2 DCs, 1 DC, 1 DC, to the end of the round. Slip stitch to join. *52 DCs total.*

Round 5: Chain 2 and add 2 DCs into the same stitch space as the chain. Add 1 DC in the next 3 stitches. Repeat the sequence: 2 DCs, 1 DC, 1 DC, 1 DC, to the end of the round. Slip stitch to join. *65 DCs total.*

Round 6: Chain 2 and add 2 DCs into the same stitch space as the chain. Add 1 DC in the next 4 stitches. Repeat the sequence: 2 DCs, 1 DC, 1 DC, 1 DC, 1 DC, to the end of the round. Slip stitch to join. *78 DCs total.*

Round 7: Chain 2 and add **1 DC** into the same stitch space as the chain. Add 1 DC in the next 5 stitches. Repeat the sequence: 2 DCs, 1 DC, 1 DC, 1 DC, 1 DC, 1 DC, to the end of the round. Slip stitch to join. *90 DCs total.*

Finish the circle: Chain 1, tighten, cut and pull through. You can weave in the tail or tuck it into the inside of the pillow when you join it to the base.

Repeat the steps above to make a second circle for the other side of the pillow.

ATTACHING THE CIRCLES

The circles will be attached to the tube of the bolster with SC stitches added from the front of the bolster. **The connecting stitches will look like piping along the edge, so you can use a contrasting color to attach these circles. I used white for black circles and black for white circles.**

Align the tube vertically with the seam side facing up and the circle at the top, right side out. Insert your hook into both loops of the first stitch at the seam on the tube and under both loops of the last stitch on the seam of the circle. Cast on with the color of your choice. Pull the loop through and chain 1.

Crocheting over the tail, SC into the same stitch as the chain and continue adding SC stitches into both loops of each stitch, through the tube and circle to the end.

Slip stitch to join to the first in the round, chain 1, tighten, cut and pull through. Weave the tail through a few stitches along the edge and pull through to the inside of the pillow.

Insert your bolster pillow foam or use a roll of thin batting cut to size. **You can also stuff with fiberfill, but over time the bolster may become lumpy.**

Attach the second circle to the opposite side of the pillow following the instructions above.

REFERENCE PHOTOS

The following reference photos are an example of some of the more complex rows in the chart. These serve as a visual guide so you can check your progress and make sure you're on the right track.

Row 3

Row 4

Row 6

Row 8

Row 9

Row 10

Skull completed.

Scarab Plant Holder

Create cute little scarab beetles for your plants! This pattern is worked in the round on a circle base and can be customized to fit most plant pots. These small plant holders are perfect for reusing and covering salsa and jelly jars, old glass candleholders or anything else you can think of to put a plant in!

Difficulty : Intermediate

Supplies for Project
- Tapestry needle
- Scissors
- Flowerpots or small containers

Hook
- H/8 (5 mm)

Gauge
- 18 stitches and 18 rows in 4" (10 cm)

Yarn Used
- Small Plant Holders
  Paintbox Cotton Aran, 100% Cotton
  - *<1 skein each (50 yards [45.5 m]) Stormy Gray, Pansy Purple, Soft Fudge*
  Ice Yarns, Rock Star, Worsted, Polyamide Blend
  - *<1 skein each (36 yards [33 m]) Blue/Green, Emerald Green, Black*

- Large Plant Holder
  Cascade Nifty Cotton, Worsted, 100% Cotton
  - *1 skein (185 yards [169 m]) Black*
  Ice Yarns, Rock Star, Worsted, Polyamide Blend
  - *½ skein (60 yards [55 m]) Light Camel*

Dimensions
- Small size fits jars 11"–12" (28–30.5 cm) around x 4" (10 cm) tall
- Large size fits pots 25" (63.5 cm) around x 7" (18 cm) tall

A Note on Yarn
This pattern uses a combination of cotton and metallic polyamide yarn, but you can also create this design using all cotton or even scrap yarn for different colored scarabs. I just had to go with metallic yarn for my scarabs! The cotton yarn also gives these holders more structure and durability.

CIRCLE BASE

Each round in the circle increases by 13 stitches, so for every round you're adding enough stitches for another scarab.

4 rounds (small plant holder) = 4 scarabs around

8 rounds (large plant holder) = 8 scarabs around

You can customize the size and shape of your plant holder by following the circle rounds below and stopping when your circle is just a little bit wider than the base of your pot or container.

If you have a pot that is tapered at the bottom (like the large flowerpot sample above), add 1 DC round with no increases to your circle (1 DC in each stitch), then continue following the increasing circle rounds below. Alternate between DC rounds with no increases and adding increasing rounds until the base fits the wide flat section of your pot.

The scarab section does not have any increases, so make sure you're choosing a flowerpot or container that has at least a 3.5" (9-cm) flat section that isn't tapered, so the scarabs will fit across without being stretched at the top.

CIRCLE ROUNDS

Start the circle with the yarn color you would like for the base of your holder. **This will be the background (color A) for the scarab section.** Chain 4 and slip stitch into the bottom of the first chain to connect.

For all rounds on the circle, work your stitches into both loops.

Round 1: Chain 2 and add 13 DCs into the center hole, crocheting over the tail.

> ### Note
> **The first 2 chains for every round do not count as a DC stitch.**

To join the round, slip stitch into both loops of the first DC in the round after the chain. (See "Stitch Placement on a Circle" [page 22].) **Repeat this step for all remaining rounds on the circle.**

Round 2: Chain 2 and add 2 DCs into the same stitch space as the chain. Add 2 DCs in each stitch to the end of the round. Slip stitch to join. *26 DCs total.*

Round 3: Chain 2 and add 2 DCs into the same stitch space as the chain. Add 1 DC in the next stitch. Repeat the sequence: 2 DCs, 1 DC, to the end of the round. Slip stitch to join. *39 DCs total.*

Round 4: Chain 2 and add 2 DCs into the same stitch space as the chain. Add 1 DC in the next 2 stitches. Repeat the sequence: 2 DCs, 1 DC, 1 DC, to the end of the round. Slip stitch to join. *52 DCs total.*

For a small plant holder, finish the circle after round 4. Chain 1 and add 1 round SC stitches into both loops. This will count as row 1 of the chart. To join the round and switch colors, follow the "Working in the Round" (pages 18–19) steps 2–6. Add round 2 (row 2 of the chart) and continue to "Following the Chart" on page 124 for 4 scarabs around.

Round 5: Chain 2 and add 2 DCs into the same stitch space as the chain. Add 1 DC in the next 3 stitches. Repeat the sequence: 2 DCs, 1 DC, 1 DC, 1 DC, to the end of the round. Slip stitch to join. *65 DCs total.*

The large plant holder sample has a DC round with no increases after round 5.

Round 6: Chain 2 and add 2 DCs into the same stitch space as the chain. Add 1 DC in the next 4 stitches. Repeat the sequence: 2 DCs, 1 DC, 1 DC, 1 DC, 1 DC, to the end of the round. Slip stitch to join. *78 DCs total.*

The large plant holder sample has a DC round with no increases after round 6.

Round 7: Chain 2 and add 2 DCs into the same stitch space as the chain. Add 1 DC in the next 5 stitches. Repeat the sequence: 2 DCs, 1 DC, 1 DC, 1 DC, 1 DC, 1 DC, to the end of the round. Slip stitch to join. *91 DCs total.*

The large plant holder sample has a DC round with no increases after round 7.

Round 8: Chain 2 and add 2 DCs into the same stitch space as the chain. Add 1 DC in the next 6 stitches. Repeat the sequence: 2 DCs, 1 DC, 1 DC, 1 DC, 1 DC, 1 DC, 1 DC, to the end of the round. Slip stitch to join. *104 DCs total.*

For a large plant holder, finish the circle after round 8. Chain 1 and add 1 round SC stitches into both loops. This will count as row 1 of the chart. To join the round and switch colors, follow the "Working in the Round" (pages 18–19) steps 2–6. Add round 2 (row 2 of the chart) and continue to "Following the Chart" on page 124 for 8 scarabs around.

Scarab Chart

13 stitches across

#	1	2	3	4	5	6	7	8	9	10	11	12	13	#
19	X	X	2	/		X	X	X		\	2	X	X	19
18				L						\				18
17	X	X		X	X	\	▽	/	X	X		X	X	17
16		X			X		X		X			X		16
15	X	X										X	X	15
14				D̄	D	X	X	X	D	D̄				14
13	X	X	X								X	X	X	13
12						\	▽	/						12
11	X	X				\	▽	/				X	X	11
10			L	X	X	X		X	X	X	L			10
9	X		X				X				X		X	9
8				X	X	X		X	X	X				8
7	X	X					X					X	X	7
6			X	\	2	X		X	2	/	X			6
5	X	X		D	D̄		X		D̄	D		X	X	5
4				L						L				4
3	X	X	D	D̄		X	X	X		D̄	D	X	X	3
2														2
1														1

☐ Color A   ▨ Color B

Stitch Key

For step-by-step instructions of special stitches, please refer to the pages listed below.

	Single Crochet	All blank boxes SC, top back loop only	
X	Double Crochet	DC in the row below of the same color	
D D̄	DC Dec Start SC	SC, 2 DCs decreased below	Page 170
D̄ D	DC Dec End SC	2 DCs decreased, SC above 2nd DC	Page 171
∟╱	Diagonal Down	Skip the next stitch, DC, SC above	Page 167
╲⌐	Diagonal Up	SC, DC below, skip the next stitch	Page 166
2 ╱	2 DCs	Skip, 2 DCs in next stitch	Page 165
╲ 2	2 DCs	2 DCs, skip the next stitch	Page 165
╲ ▽ ╱	Triangle	Skip, DC, SC above, DC below in same stitch, skip	Page 176

FOLLOWING THE CHART

Your first round is color A (background), and second round color B (scarab color), as indicated in the numbered column of the chart.

All remaining rounds will follow the "Working in the Round" instructions (page 18) for joining and switching colors.

After completing rounds 1 and 2, begin following the chart from row 3. Follow across all 13 stitches in the row and repeat these 13 stitches again to your desired size (4 scarabs for small, 8 scarabs for large). **The number of scarabs around will be the same number of rounds in the circle base, not including any rounds with no increases.**

Follow the chart from rows 3–19. To finish the top of the edge, add 1 round of SC stitches into both loops using color A. For a wider edge at the top, using color A only, add 1 round of SC stitches (back loop only) and 1 round of overlay DC stitches. Repeat as needed to reach the top of your flowerpot or container. Add 1 more round of SC stitches into both loops and join from the back.

To end after the join, chain 1, tighten, cut about a 4" (10-cm) tail and pull through. Weave the tail end on the inside at the seam so it is next to the yarn from the last color change. Cut the other color and leave about a 4" (10-cm) tail end. Tie both tail ends together with a square knot. Weave in all ends on the inside.

REFERENCE PHOTOS

The following reference photos are an example of some of the more complex rows in the chart. These serve as a visual guide so you can check your progress and make sure you're on the right track.

Row 4

Row 5

Row 6

Row 11

Row 12

Row 14

Scarab completed.

The Victorian Pillow

Create an ultra-fancy pillow with intricate floral medallions, reminiscent of Victorian damask-style wallpaper and textiles. This pattern is worked flat with border stitches and the front and back panels are attached together with faux fur yarn trim.

Difficulty: Advanced

Supplies for Project
- Scissors
- Fiberfill or pillow insert

Hooks
- H/8 (5 mm)
- J/10 (5.75 mm) for trim

Gauge
- 20 stitches and 20 rows in 4" (10 cm)

Yarn Used
Malabrigo Rios, Worsted, 100% Merino Wool
  - 2 skeins (300 yards [274.5 m]) Sabiduria
  - 2 skeins (300 yards [274.5 m]) Pearl

Sirdar Alpine, 100% Polyester
  - 1 skein (30 yards [27.5 m]) Mink

Dimensions
- About 13" x 13" (33 x 33 cm)

Victorian Left Chart

Victorian Right Chart

34 stitches in repeat

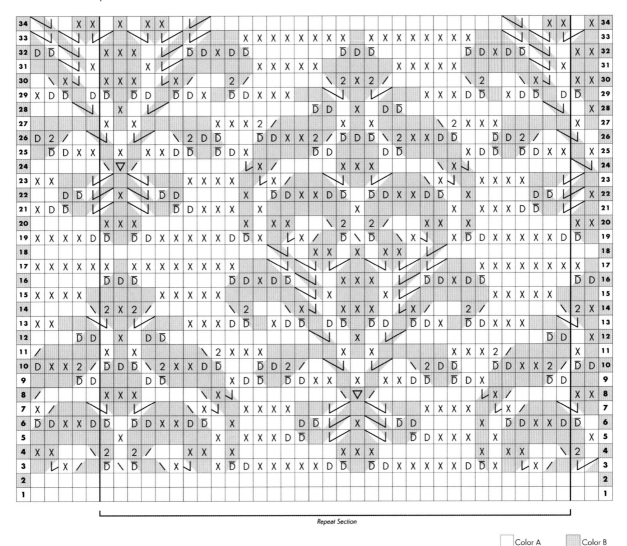

Repeat Section

Color A   Color B

Stitch Key

For step-by-step instructions of special stitches, please refer to the pages listed below.

	Single Crochet	*All blank boxes SC, top back loop only*	
X	**Double Crochet**	*DC in the row below of the same color*	
⌐	**Diagonal Down**	*Skip the next stitch, DC, SC above*	*Page 167*
⌐	**Diagonal Up**	*SC, DC below, skip the next stitch*	*Page 166*
⌐X╱	**Double Diagonal Down**	*Skip the next stitch, DC, DC, SC above*	*Page 169*
╲X⌐	**Double Diagonal Up**	*SC, DC below, DC, skip the next stitch*	*Page 168*
D D̄	**DC Dec Start SC**	*SC, 2 DCs decreased below*	*Page 170*
D̄ D	**DC Dec End SC**	*2 DCs decreased, SC above 2nd DC*	*Page 171*
╲ 2	**2 DCs**	*2 DCs, skip the next stitch*	*Page 165*
2 ╱	**2 DCs**	*Skip, 2 DCs in next stitch*	*Page 165*
╲▽╱	**Triangle**	*Skip, DC, SC above, DC below in same stitch, skip*	*Page 176*
D̄╲D̄	**DC Dec Centered**	*SC, start decrease below, skip, finish decrease, SC above*	*Page 174*
D̄ D D̄	**DC Dec 3 Together**	*SC, 3 DCs decreased below, SC above 3rd DC*	*Page 173*

FOUNDATION CHAIN

When calculating your foundation chain, use **multiples of 34 chains plus 1**.

To calculate your foundation chain, start with the number of full medallions you would like across, multiplied by 34, plus 1, plus 2 more for the border stitches.

For 2 medallions across as shown in the example: 2 x 34 + 1 + 2 = 71

Begin your foundation chain in color A (**background color**) with 71 chains, or the appropriate stitch count for your specific size.

FOLLOWING THE CHARTS

Your first row is color A (background), and your second row is color B (medallion color), as indicated in the numbered column of the charts.

Row 1: Chain 1 and SC into the second chain from the hook. SC the entire row. Chain 1, pull down to tighten, cut a 2"–3" (5–7.5-cm) tail and pull through.

Row 2: Start with a border stitch and add SC stitches for the entire row, up to the last stitch. Finish with a border stitch and cut a 2"–3" (5–7.5-cm) tail.

Begin following the Victorian Right Chart from row 3. Start with the first 2 stitches in the row before the repeat section. Follow across all 34 stitches in the repeat section. **For a larger size with 3 or more full medallions across, repeat those 34 stitches in the repeat section again to your desired size.** Follow across the last 5 stitches in the Victorian Right Chart, and continue across all 28 stitches in the Victorian Left Chart.

Left-handed: Begin with the Victorian Left Chart and continue to the Victorian Right Chart following the instructions for the repeat section above. Finish the row with the last 2 stitches in the row after the repeat section.

Note

Some special stitches at the end of the Victorian Right Chart continue on the Victorian Left Chart (end of rows 7, 8, 10, 11 and 26).

Follow the charts from rows 3–34, start the chart over from row 3 and finish with row 33. **For a taller pillow, you can repeat rows 3–34 as many times as you like, and finish with row 33.**

Repeat the steps above to create a second pillow panel. You can reverse the colors for the second panel or make it in the same colors as the front.

Back panel with colors reversed

Completed pillow panel with 2 full medallions across.

ATTACHING THE PANELS

Align both panels right side out, back sides together.

In the bottom right border stitch (bottom left for left-handed crocheters), secure the end of the fur yarn through both panels with a knot. Insert your hook into the border stitch and pull through a loop. Chain 2.

Working through both panels, DC in between **every other border stitch**, tucking the tail ends toward the inside as you're crocheting.

Chain 3 at the corner and start your next DC in the following stitch. Add DCs in every other stitch along the top. Chain 3 at the corner. Continue adding DCs under every other border stitch, tucking the tail ends toward the inside.

Use a pillow insert or stuff with fill. **The overlay stitches prevent any fill from coming through the stitches, so you can directly stuff the pillow without using an insert.**

To close the bottom, chain 3 and continue adding DCs in every other stitch to the end. Chain 3 and slip stitch at the base to join. Weave your tails along the tight stitches at the base and pull the tail through to the inside of the pillow to hide it.

REFERENCE PHOTOS

The following reference photos are an example of some of the more complex rows in the chart. These serve as a visual guide so you can check your progress and make sure you're on the right track. These photos show 1 repeat on the right side. **Rows 19–34 are the same as rows 3–18, shifted over by half.**

Row 3

Row 3 - DC Dec Center

Row 4

Row 5

Row 6

Row 7

Row 8 & 24 Center

Row 9

Row 10

Row 13

Row 14

Row 16

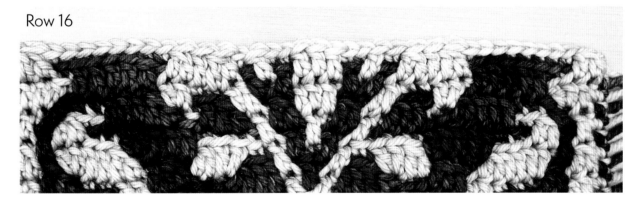

Row 16 Center & Row 32

Row 17

Row 19

Medallion completed.

On Fire Table Runner

Add some fiery drama to your dining space with this ultra-hot table runner pattern. You can easily create your own gradient of solid colors or use a gradient yarn to create the flames. This pattern is worked flat with border stitches and extra tassels added to the tail ends to create fringe.

Difficulty: Advanced

Supplies for Project
- Standard ruler
- Scissors
- Tapestry needle

Hook
- H/8 (5 mm)

Gauge
- 18 stitches and 18 rows in 4" (10 cm)

Yarn Used
Cascade Nifty Cotton, Worsted, 100% Cotton
- 2 skeins (300 yards [274.5 m]) Black
- 1 skein (125 yards [114.5 m]) Marigold (orange)
- <1 skein (90 yards [82.5 m]) Blue
- <1 skein (50 yards [45.5 m]) Blue Iris (periwinkle)
- <1 skein (50 yards [45.5 m]) Grape (purple)

Dimensions
- 9.5" x 40" (24 x 101.5 cm) (9.5" x 46" [24 x 117 cm] with 3" [7.5-cm] tassels)

A Note on Yarn
This table runner was made using a solid color for each color A row, arranged in a gradient from blue to orange. To recreate this design use blue for rows 1 and 3, periwinkle for row 5, purple for row 7, and orange for rows 9, 11 and 13.

On Fire Chart 1

15 stitches in repeat

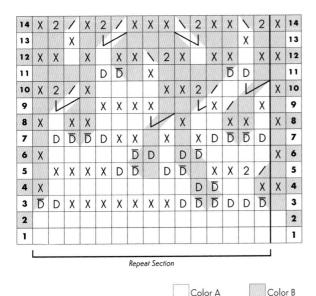

Repeat Section

☐ Color A   ▨ Color B

On Fire Chart 2

15 stitches in repeat

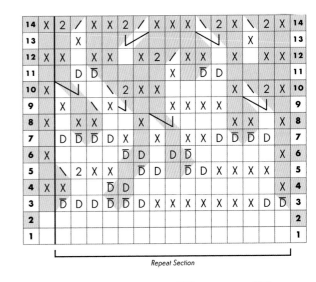

Repeat Section

☐ Color A   ▨ Color B

Stitch Key

For step-by-step instructions of special stitches, please refer to the pages listed below.

	Single Crochet	All blank boxes SC, top back loop only	
X	Double Crochet	DC in the row below of the same color	
D̄ D	DC Dec End SC	2 DCs decreased, SC above 2nd DC	Page 171
D D̄	DC Dec Start SC	SC, 2 DCs decreased below	Page 170
2 /	2 DCs	Skip, 2 DCs in next stitch	Page 165
\ 2	2 DCs	2 DCs, skip the next stitch	Page 165
⌐/	Diagonal Down	Skip the next stitch, DC, SC above	Page 167
\⌐	Diagonal Up	SC, DC below, skip the next stitch	Page 166
\X⌐	Double Diagonal Up	SC, DC below, DC, skip the next stitch	Page 168
⌐X/	Double Diagonal Down	Skip the next stitch, DC, DC, SC above	Page 169

FOUNDATION CHAIN

When calculating your foundation chain, use **multiples of 15 chains plus 1**.

The foundation chain is calculated by the number of repeats across, multiplied by 15, plus 1, plus 2 more for the border stitches.

For a 40" (101.5-cm) table runner (11 repeats): 11 x 15 + 1 + 2 = 168

Begin your foundation chain in color A (**flame color**) with 168 chains.

FOLLOWING THE CHARTS

Your first row is color A (flame color), and your second row is color B (background color), as indicated in the numbered column of the charts.

Row 1: Chain 1 and SC into the second chain from the hook. SC the entire row. Chain 1, pull down to tighten, cut a 3" (7.5-cm) tail and pull through.

Row 2: Start with a border stitch and add SC stitches for the entire row, up to the last stitch. Finish with a border stitch and cut a 3" (7.5-cm) tail. **All remaining rows will start and end with a border stitch.**

Begin following **On Fire Chart 1** from row 3. Start with the first stitch in the row before the repeat section. Follow across all 15 stitches in the repeat section and repeat those 15 stitches in the repeat section 11 times total, or to your desired size. Follow the chart from rows 3–14.

Begin following **On Fire Chart 2** from row 1. Follow across all 15 stitches in the repeat section and repeat those 15 stitches in the repeat section 11 times total, or to your desired size. Finish the row with the last stitch in the row after the repeat section. Follow the chart from rows 1–14.

For a table runner 3 flame sections tall, repeat On Fire Chart 1, rows 1–14. Finish with 1 row of SC stitches in the top back loops with color B.

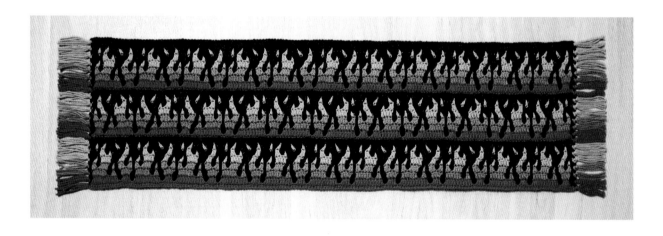

ADDING FRINGE

To hide the tail ends and create fringe to match the flame gradient, begin by weaving in all color B tail ends. Cut 6" (15-cm)-long strands of yarn, 2 for each color A border stitch.

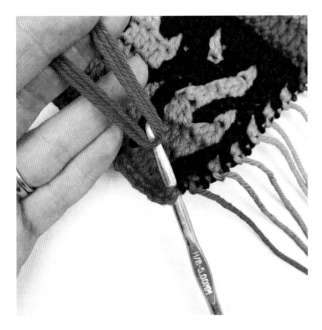

For an even number of tassels on both sides, add 3 strands folded in half to the very first border stitch on the bottom right, matching the color of the first border stitch. Insert your hook under the first border stitch on the bottom right side of the table runner. Hook 3 strips of yarn folded in half and pull through a loop. Pull all 6 tails through the loop. Pull the short tails to tighten.

Continue adding tassels, 2 strands folded in half (**matching the border stitch color**) between every other border stitch, and add 1 matching tail end into each tassel for all remaining border stitches.

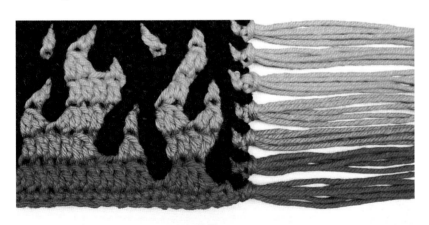

Block your finished table runner on a blocking mat and trim any excess yarn fringe so it is even on both ends.

REFERENCE PHOTOS

*The following reference photos are an example of some of the more complex rows in the **On Fire Chart 1**. These serve as a visual guide so you can check your progress and make sure you're on the right track. **On Fire Chart 2 is a mirror image of On Fire Chart 1.***

Row 3

Row 4

Row 5

Row 6

Row 7

Row 9

Row 10

Row 11

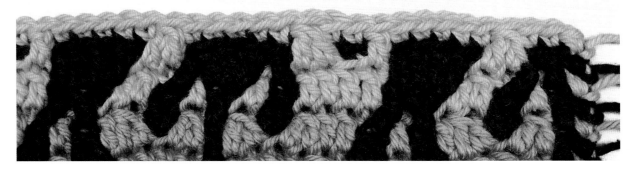

Chart 1 completed.

Sun & Moon Pillow

Create a dynamic sun and moon pillow inspired by the designs on those mysterious and iconic spirit boards! This pattern is worked flat with border stitches and the front and back panels are attached together from the inside. The large format chart is broken down into six easy-to-read sections, and although it may look intimidating, if you just take it row by row it is so enjoyable to watch the design reveal itself!

You can also use this pattern to create a large place mat or even a wall hanging with just one panel. For instructions on finishing the edges, see Ends & Tassels (pages 25–29).

Difficulty: Advanced

Supplies for Project
- Scissors
- Tapestry needle
- Fiberfill or pillow insert

Hook
- H/8 (5 mm)

Gauge
- 19 stitches and 19 rows in 4" (10 cm)

Yarn Used
Cascade 220 Superwash Merino, Worsted, 100% Merino Wool
- 1 skein (208 yards [190 m]) Black
- 1 skein (170 yards [155.5 m]) Tuffet (beige)
- 1 skein (208 yards [190 m]) Navy
- 1 skein (170 yards [155.5 m]) Flint Gray

Dimensions
- 18" x 13" (45 x 33 cm) (about 16" x 12" [40.5 x 30 cm] stuffed)

A Note on Yarn
I recommend using a light worsted or DK weight yarn for this project. A medium worsted weight yarn will end up producing a much larger pillow than the dimensions listed. For more information on gauge and yarn, see page 24.

FOUNDATION CHAIN
Begin your foundation chain in color A (**background color**) with 86 chains.

This stitch count includes the 2 border stitches for the beginning and end of the row.

FOLLOWING THE CHARTS (PAGES 152—156)
Your first row is color A (background), and your second row is color B (sun and moon color), as indicated in the numbered column of the charts.

Row 1: Chain 1 and SC into the second chain from the hook. SC the entire row. Chain 1, pull down to tighten, cut a 2"–3" (5–7.5-cm) tail and pull through.

Row 2: Start with a border stitch and add SC stitches for the entire row, up to the last stitch. Finish with a border stitch and cut a 2"–3" (5–7.5-cm) tail.

The bottom half of the pillow will follow across Sun & Moon Charts 1, 2 and 3 from right to left. **(Left-handed crocheters follow from left to right across Sun & Moon Charts 3, 2 and 1.)**

Start Sun & Moon Chart 1 from row 3 and follow across all 28 stitches. Continue the row following across Sun & Moon Chart 2 (**28 stitches**) and across Sun & Moon Chart 3 (**28 stitches**). You will have 84 stitches across the row. Follow across all 3 charts from rows 3–32.

For the top half of the pillow, follow across Sun & Moon Charts 4, 5 and 6 from right to left. **(Left-handed crocheters follow from left to right across Sun & Moon Charts 6, 5 and 4.)** Start Sun & Moon Chart 4 from row 33 and follow across all 28 stitches. Continue the row following across Sun & Moon Chart 5 (**28 stitches**) and across Sun & Moon Chart 6 (**28 stitches**). You will have 84 stitches across the row. Follow across all 3 charts from rows 33–61. Finish with 1 row of SC stitches in both loops with color A.

Note

Some special stitches at the top and bottom of the sun rays are split and continue on to the next chart.

Sun & Moon Chart 2—end of row 4 and 8 (Triangles)

Sun & Moon Chart 5—end of row 56 (DC Dec Centered) and 60 (DC Dec 3 Together)

Repeat the steps above to create a second pillow panel. You can make an identical panel, reverse the colors or use 2 new colors. **If you're using 2 new colors for the back, make sure all 4 colors go well together because you may be able to still see the edges of the back of the pillow along the sides and the top.**

Sun & Moon Chart 1 — Bottom Right

32	X	X					Ð	D	X	\	2	X	X	X	X	X	X	X	X	X	X	X	X	X	X				32
31		Ð	D	X	X	X	X				\													X	X	X	31
30					Ð	D	X	X	D	Ð	\	2	X	X	X	X	X	X	X	X	X	X	X			30
29	X	X	X	X	X	D	Ð				\												X	X	X	29
28						\		X	X	X	X	X	X	X	X	X	X	X	X	X	X				28
27		X	X	X	X	X	X	X												Ð	D	X	X	27
26					Ð	D	X	X	X	X	X	X	X	X	X	X	X	X	X	X			26
25				X	X	X													X	X	X	X	25
24				\	2	X	X	X	X	X	X	X	X	X	X	X	X	2	/				24
23	X	X	X	X	X	X	X	X	D	Ð										X	X	X	X	X	23
22				\	2	X	X	X	X	X	X	X	X	X	2	/						22
21	X	X	X	X	X	X	X	X										X	X	X	X	X	X	21
20				X	X	X	X	X	X	X	X	X	X	X	2	/					20
19	X	X	X	X	X	X	2	/								Ð	D	X	X	X	X	X	X	X	19
18			Ð	D	X	X	X	X	X	X	X	X	X	X	X						18
17	X	X	X	X	2	/									Ð	D	X	X	X	X	X	X	X	17
16		Ð	D	X	X	X	X	X	X	X	X	X	X	X	2	/					16
15										Ð	D	X	X	X	X		X	X	X	X	15
14	X	X	X	X	X	X	X	X	X	X	X	X	X	2	/			X			14
13									Ð	D	X	X	X	X				X	X	13
12	X	X	X	X	X	X	X	X	X	X	2	/					X			12
11					Ð	D	X	X	X	X	X		X	X	X		X	X	X	X	11
10										X							10
9	X	X	X	X	X	X	X	X	X	X	X	X		X		X		X	X	X	X	X	X	9
8								\		X		\					8
7	X	X	X	X	X	X	X	X		X	X	X				X	X	X	X	X	7
6					X			\/		X		\				6
5		X	X	X	X	X	X		X	X	X		X		X		X	X	X	X	X	X	X	5
4				X					X					4
3			X	X	X	X		X	X	X	X	X	X		X	X	X	X	X	X	X	X	3
2													2
1													1

Color A   Color B

Sun & Moon Chart 3 — Bottom Left

#																								#
32	X						X		X	X	X	X	X	X	X	X	X	X	X	X		X	X	32
31			╲	2	X	X	X	X		X											X			31
30				╲↓			↓			X	X	X	X	X	X	X	X	X	X		X	X		30
29	X	X	X	D	D̄			D̄	D	X									╲↓					29
28								X	X	X	X	X	X	X	X	X	X		X	X				28
27	X	X	X	X	X	X	2	/			╲↓								╲↓					27
26					↳	X	/		X		X	X	X	X	X	X	X	X	X	X	X	D	D̄	26
25	X	X	X	X	2	/		D̄	D	X	D	D̄	╲↓								2	/		25
24			↳	X	/				X		X	X	X	X	X	X	X	X	X	2	/			24
23	2	/			D̄	D	X	X	2	/		D	D̄						D̄	D	X	X		23
22	╲↓		╲	X	↳			↳	X	/			╲	2	X	X	X	X	X					22
21	D̄	D	X	D	D̄				↳			╲↓												21
20						↳			╲	X	↳	╲	2	X	X	X	X	X	X	X	X			20
19	X	X	X	X	X	X	X	X		X	X	D	D̄		D	D̄								19
18							X			X				╲	2	X	X	X						18
17				X	X	2	/		X	X	X	X		X			╲↓							17
16						2	/			↳		↳			╲	X	↳							16
15			X	X	X	2	/		2	/		D̄	D		X	X	D	D̄		X				15
14				D̄	D	X	↳	X	/			X				X		2	/					14
13		X	X	X	2	/			D̄	D	X	X	X		X	X	X		X		X	X	X	13
12					2	/							╲↓			X		D	D̄					12
11	X	X	X	X	X	X	D̄	D	X	X	X	X	X	X		X	2	/		D	D̄		X	X	11
10												X	↳	X	/			╲↓						10
9				X	X	X	X	X	X	X	X	2	/			D̄	D	X	X			X		9
8									X	2	/								╲	▽				8
7						X	X	X	X		D̄	D	X	X	X	X	2	/						7
6								X								X	X							6
5							X	X	D	D̄	X	X	X	X	X	X	X	X						5
4															╲	▽								4
3							X	X	X	X	X	X	X	X	X	X	X							3
2																								2
1																								1

Color A (shaded)   Color B (white)

Sun & Moon Chart 2 — Bottom Middle

32	X	X	X	X	X	X	X	X	X	X	X	X	X	X	X	X		X												X	X		**32**
31												X		X	X	X	X	2	/														**31**
30	X	X	X	X	X	X	X	X	X	X	X	X			╲					╲													**30**
29												X	D	D̄					D̄	D	X	X	X	X									**29**
28	X			X	X	X	X	X	X	X	X	X									╲	2	X	X	X								**28**
27	╚										╚						╲	2	X	X	X												**27**
26	D̄	D	X	X	X	X	X	X	X	X	X	X		X		╲	X	╲															**26**
25		╚									╚	D̄	D	X	D	D̄		╲	2	X	X	X	X										**25**
24		╲	2	X	X	X	X	X	X	X	X		X			╲	X	╚					╲	2	X		**24**
23	X	D	D̄							D̄	D		╲	2	X	X	X	D	D̄				╲	2	X		**23**
22				X	X	X	X	X	2	/		╲	X	╚				╚	X	/		╲		╚		**22**
21							╚						╚				D̄	D	X	D	D̄	X		**21**
20	X	X	X	X	X	X	X	2	/	╚	X	/		╚																			**20**
19					D̄	D		D̄	D	X	X		X	X	X	╲	2	X	X	X	X	X		**19**
18		X	X	X	2	/				X			X		╚								**18**
17			╚			X		X	X	X	X	╲	2	X	X	X	╲	2	X	X	X		**17**
16			╚	X	/		╚		╚		╲	2				╲	X	╚		**16**
15			X		D̄	D	X	X		D	D̄	╲	2		╲	2	X	X	D	D̄		**15**
14		╲	2		X			X		╲	X	╚	X	D	D̄		╲	2	X	X	X		**14**
13	X	X		X		X	X	X		X	X	X	D	D̄		╲	2	X	X	D	D̄		**13**
12		D̄	D		X			╚				╲	2			╲	2		**12**
11	X		D̄	D		╲	2	X		X	X	X	X	X	X	X	D	D̄	X	X	X	X	X	D	D̄		**11**
10	╚			╲	X	╚		X																	**10**
9		X	X	X	D	D̄		╲	2	X	X	X	X	X	X	X	X	X	X	X	X	X	X		**9**
8	/				╲	2	X																		**8**
7	╲	2	X	X	X	X	X	D	D̄		X	X	X	X	X							X	X	X		**7**
6	X					X																			**6**
5		X	X	X	X	X	X	X	X	D̄	D	X	X												**5**
4	/																								**4**
3	X	X	X	X	X	X	X	X	X	X	X														**3**
2																									**2**
1																									**1**

Color A   Color B

Sun & Moon Chart 5 — Top Middle

Color A | Color B

Sun & Moon Chart 4 — Top Right

61					X	X	X	X		X	X	X	X	X	X		X		X	X	X	X	X	X	X	X	61
60							X								X												60
59		X	X	X	X	X	X	X				X	X	X		X		X		X	X	X	X	X	X	X	59
58							X							↘		X	↙										58
57	X	X	X	X	X	X	X	X	X	X		X	X	X							X	X	X	X	X	X	57
56												↙		X		↘											56
55	X	X	X	X	X	X	X	X	X	X	X	X	X		X		X		X	X	X	X	X	X		55
54														X													54
53						↘	2	X	X	X	X	X		X	X	X		X	X	X							53
52	X	X	X	X	X	X	X	X	X	X	X	X	D	D̄							X						52
51									↘	2	X	X	X	X							X	X					51
50	X	X	X	X	X	X	X	X	X	X	X	X	X	D	D̄					X							50
49										↘	2	X	X	X		X	X	X	X								49
48			↘	2	X	X	X	X	X	X	X	X	X	X	D	D̄											48
47	X	X	X	X	D	D̄								↘	2	X	X	X	X	X	X						47
46			↘	2	X	X	X	X	X	X	X	X	X	X													46
45	X	X	X	X	X	D	D̄								↘	2	X	X	X	X	X						45
44					X	X	X	X	X	X	X	X	X	X	X	D	D̄										44
43	X	X	X	X	X	X	X										X	X	X	X	X						43
42					X	X	X	X	X	X	X	X	X	X	X	X	D	D̄									42
41	X	X	X	X	X	X												X	X	X	X						41
40					X				↘	2	X	X	X	X	X	X	D	D̄									40
39				X	X	D	D̄		↙	↘									X	X	X						39
38				↘	↙		↘	2	D	D̄	X	X	X	X	X	X	X	X									38
37			X	X	X	X	X	X		D	D̄							↘	2	X	X						37
36					D̄	D		↘	2	X	X	X	X	X	X	X	X										36
35	X	X	X	X	X	X	X		X		↙	↘							X	X	X						35
34				D̄	D			X	X	X	X	X	X	X	X	X											34
33		↘	2	X	X	X	X												X	X	X						33

Color A Color B

Sun & Moon Chart 6—Top Left

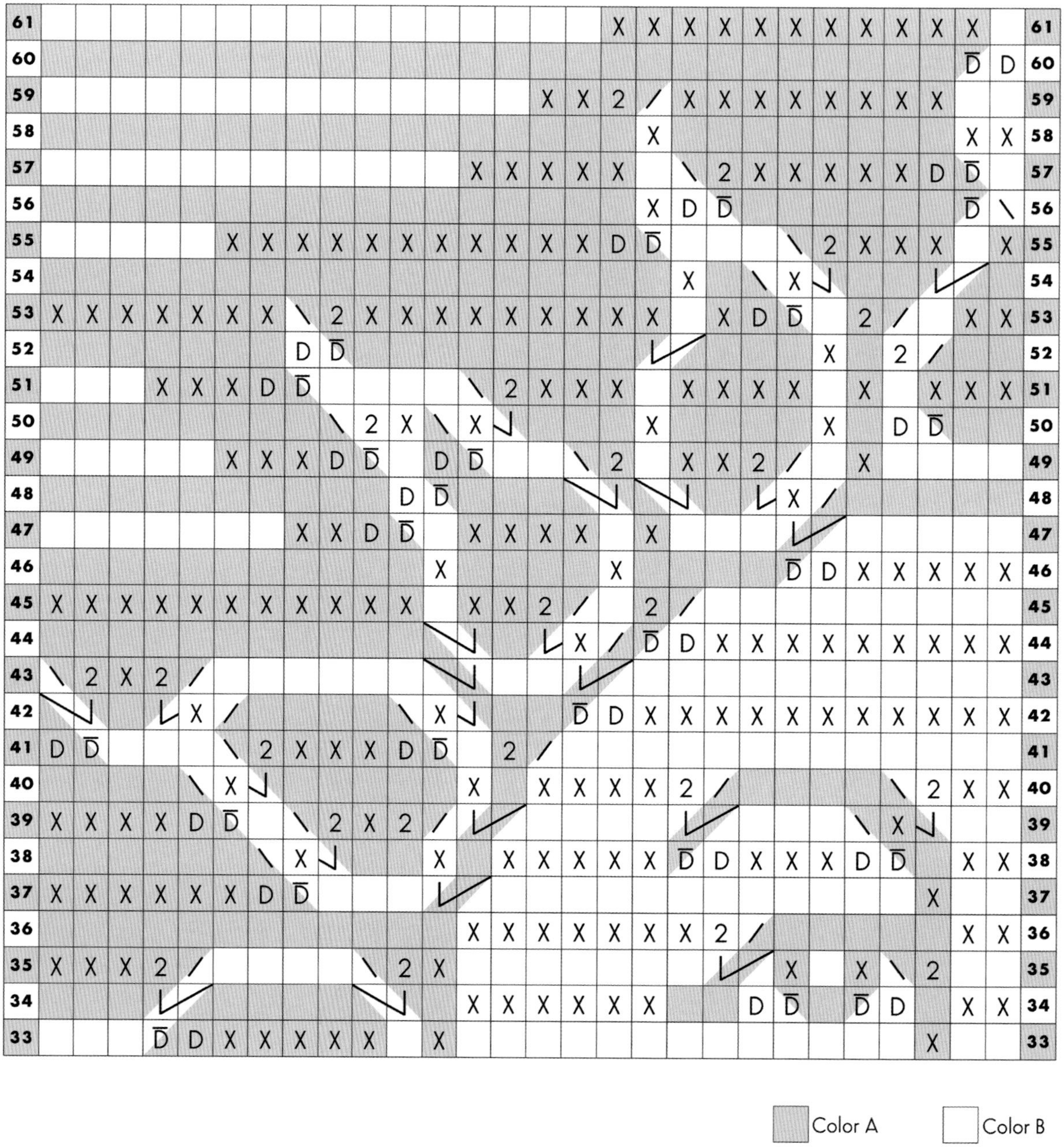
Color A
Color B

Stitch Key

For step-by-step instructions of special stitches, please refer to the pages listed below.

	Single Crochet	*All blank boxes SC, top back loop only*	
X	**Double Crochet**	*DC in the row below of the same color*	
⌄	**Diagonal Down**	Skip the next stitch, DC, SC above	*Page 167*
⌄	**Diagonal Up**	*SC, DC below, skip the next stitch*	*Page 166*
⌄X⌄	**Double Diagonal Down**	*Skip the next stitch, DC, DC, SC above*	*Page 169*
⌄X⌄	**Double Diagonal Up**	*SC, DC below, DC, skip the next stitch*	*Page 168*
DD̄	**DC Dec Start SC**	*SC, 2 DCs decreased below*	*Page 170*
D̄D	**DC Dec End SC**	*2 DCs decreased, SC above 2nd DC*	*Page 171*
\ 2	**2 DCs**	*2 DCs, skip the next stitch*	*Page 165*
2 /	**2 DCs**	*Skip, 2 DCs in next stitch*	*Page 165*
\▽/	**Triangle**	*Skip, DC, SC above, DC below in same stitch, skip*	*Page 176*
D̄\D̄	**DC Dec Centered**	*SC, start decrease below, skip, finish decrease, SC above*	*Page 174*
D̄D̄	**DC Dec 3 Together**	*SC, 3 DCs decreased below, SC above 3rd DC*	*Page 173*

ATTACHING THE PANELS

Align your 2 panels together, right sides facing. Choose a yarn that matches the background color of either panel and secure your yarn with a knot through both panels of the bottom right corner border stitch. Insert your hook into the first stitch and begin adding slip stitches through both panels, under each of the border stitches on the right side, across all stitches at the top (both loops) and between the border stitches on the left side. **(For left-handed crocheters, start from the bottom left corner and work your way across the left side, top and right side.)**

Chain 1, tighten and cut a tail end 1–1.5 yards (91–137 cm) long. Pull the tail end all the way through the hook. **This reserved yarn will be used for stitching the bottom of the pillow closed.**

Flip your pillow case right side out and insert your pillow or stuff with fiberfill. Thread a tapestry needle on to the long tail end and whip stitch the bottom closed. Tie and secure, and then weave in your tail across the stitches along the bottom and into the inside of the pillow.

REFERENCE PHOTOS

The following reference photos are an example of some of the more complex rows in the chart. These serve as a visual guide so you can check your progress and make sure you're on the right track. The sun reference photos show Sun & Moon Charts 2 and 3 together and Sun & Moon Charts 5 and 6 together. The sun rays are mirrored on the right and left and the top and bottom.

Row 9 - Sun

Row 10 - Sun

Row 12 - Moon

Row 12 - Sun

Row 14 - Chart 2

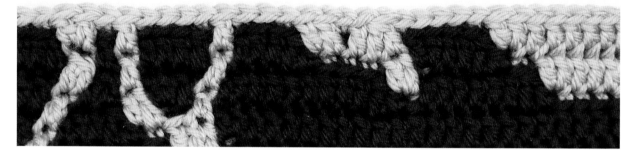

Row 15 - Chart 2

Row 16 - Chart 2

160 × Dark & Dramatic Mosaic Crochet

Row 30 - Moon

Row 32 - Moon

Row 56 - Sun

Row 60 - Sun

Special Stitches

Beyond standard SC and DC mosaic crochet stitches, this section will cover all of the special stitches that create different curves, angles and points. This section will walk you step-by-step through each of the stitches so you can learn how to read the symbols in the charts of the patterns. All of the symbols in the charts are read from right to left, and crocheted in the same direction—though if you're left-handed, you'll read and crochet them from left to right.

You'll also find information on how to handle hidden stitches and special stitch combinations that you'll come across in some of the intermediate and advanced patterns.

Stitch Guide

BOBBLES B

Bobble stitches are 2 DCs decreased together in the same stitch. This will make the stitch space a bit larger than a regular SC. **Please note that this is the ONLY TIME you will be adding DCs into a top row, rather than into the row below.**

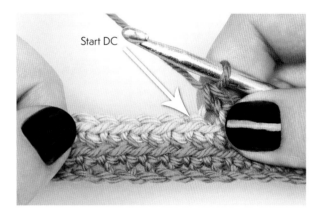

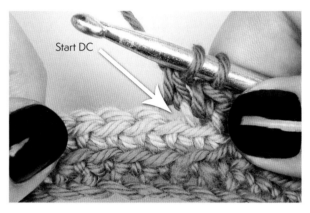

1. Start your DC in the next stitch and work the stitch until you have 2 loops left on your hook.

2. Yarn over and start your next DC back into the same hole, working the stitch until you have 3 loops left on your hook.

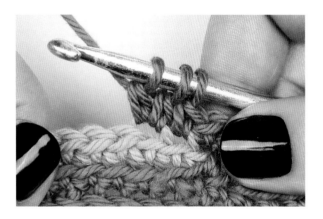

3. Yarn over and pull through all 3 loops. This will connect the two DCs into one stitch.

Bobble completed.

Left-Handed: Follow the same steps listed above.

2 DCS IN THE SAME STITCH

A "2" in the chart indicates 2 DCs into the same stitch. Be sure to skip a stitch as indicated in the chart to accommodate for the doubles.

(2 stitches will be skipped in the back)

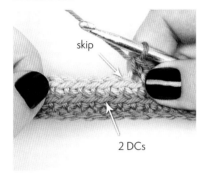

Left-Handed: Start with 2 DCs in the next stitch; skip the following stitch.

1. This sequence starts with a skip. Add 2 DCs into the following stitch.

Two DCs in the same stitch after a skip.

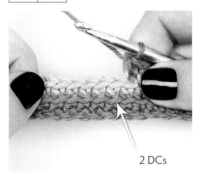

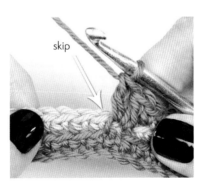

1. This sequence starts with a 2. Add 2 DCs into the next stitch.

2. Skip the next stitch.

2 DCs in the same stitch followed by a skip. **Image shown with 1 SC in the next stitch.**

Left-Handed: Skip the next stitch, add 2 DCs in the following stitch.

DIAGONALS

DIAGONAL UP

Start your next stitch with a SC, then a DC directly below it. Skip the next stitch.

(1 stitch will be skipped in the back)

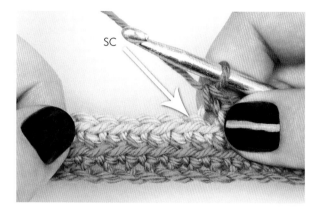

1. SC in the next stitch.

2. Add a DC directly below the SC stitch.

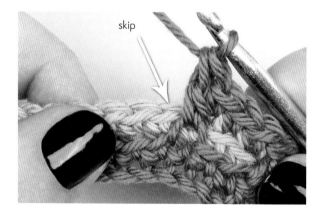

3. Skip the next stitch.

Diagonal Up completed. **Image shows 1 SC added after diagonal.**

> **Left-Handed:** Skip the next stitch, add a DC, SC directly above the DC.

DIAGONAL DOWN

Skip the next stitch and DC into the following stitch. Add a SC directly above the DC.

(1 stitch will be skipped in the back)

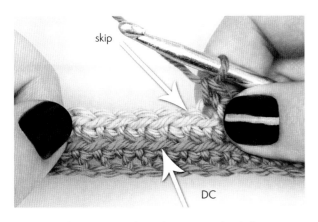

1. Skip the next stitch and DC into the following stitch.

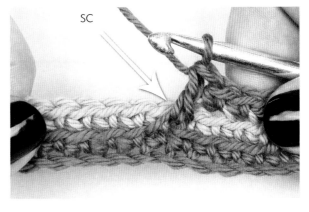

2. Add a SC directly above the DC.

Diagonal Down completed.

> **Left-Handed:** Start your next stitch with a SC, then a DC directly below it. Skip the next stitch.

DOUBLE DIAGONALS

The DCs between the skip and SC will make all DCs in this sequence diagonal. These stitches are just like diagonal stitches split in half with an extra DC in the middle.

(2 stitches will be skipped in the back)

DOUBLE DIAGONAL UP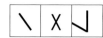

Start with a SC, and add a DC directly below. Add a DC into the next stitch and skip the next stitch.

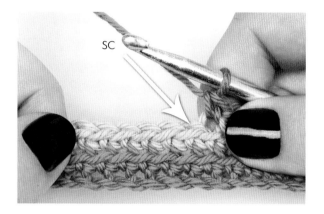

1. Start with a SC in the next stitch.

2. Add a DC directly below the SC.

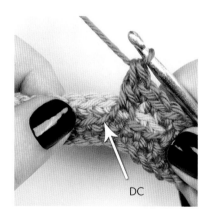

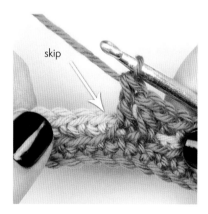

3. Add a DC in the next stitch.

4. Skip the next stitch.

Double Diagonal Up completed.
Image shows 1 SC added after the skip.

> **Left-Handed:** Skip the next stitch and add a DC into the following stitch. Add a DC into the next stitch and finish with a SC directly above the last DC.

DOUBLE DIAGONAL DOWN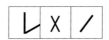

Skip the next stitch and add a DC into the following stitch. Add a DC into the next stitch and finish with a SC directly above the last DC.

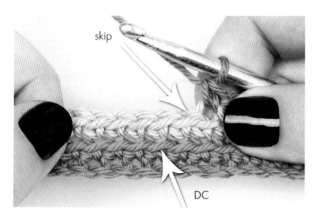

1. Skip the next stitch. Add a DC into the following stitch.

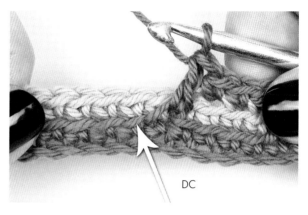

2. Add a DC into the next stitch.

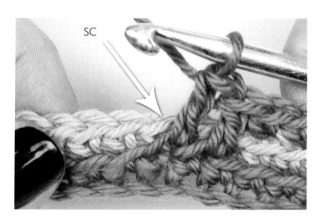

3. Add a SC directly above the last DC stitch.

Double Diagonal Down completed.

Left-Handed: Start with a SC, and add a DC directly below. Add a DC into the next stitch. Skip the next stitch.

DC DECREASES

All "D"s with a line above represent a SC stitch added above them.

DC DECREASE START SC

SC in the next stitch and start a DC directly below it. Start a DC in the next stitch. Finish by pulling through all 3 loops.

(1 stitch will be skipped in the back)

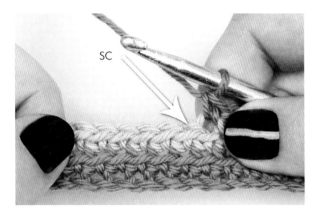

1. Start with a SC in the next stitch.

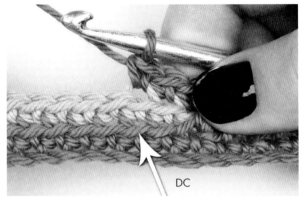

2. Begin adding a DC stitch directly below the SC. Work the stitch until you have 2 loops left on your hook.

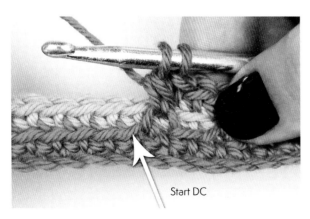

3. Yarn over and start your next DC in the next stitch, working the stitch until you have 3 loops left on your hook.

4. Yarn over and pull through all 3 loops. This will connect both DCs into one stitch.

DC Decrease Start SC completed.

> **Left-Handed:** Start a DC in the next stitch. Start another DC in the following stitch. Finish by pulling through all 3 loops. Add a SC directly above the last DC stitch.

DC DECREASE END SC

Start a DC in the next stitch. Start another DC in the following stitch. Finish by pulling through all 3 loops. Add a SC directly above the last DC stitch.

(1 stitch will be skipped in the back)

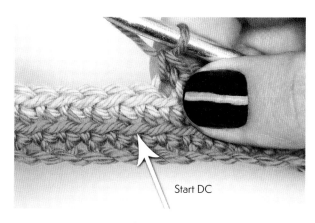

Start DC

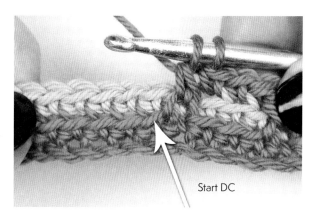

Start DC

1. Start your DC in the next stitch and stop when you have 2 loops left on your hook.

2. Yarn over and start your next DC in the next stitch, working the stitch until you have 3 loops left on your hook.

DC DECREASE END SC (continued)

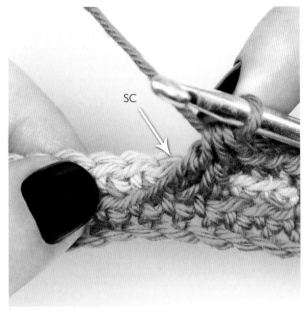

3. Yarn over and pull through all 3 loops. This will connect both DCs into one stitch.

4. Finish the sequence with a SC added directly above the last DC stitch.

Left-Handed: SC in the next stitch and start a DC directly below it. Start a DC in the next stitch. Finish by pulling through all 3 loops.

DC Decrease End SC completed.

DC DECREASE 3 TOGETHER $\overline{\text{D}}$ | D | $\overline{\text{D}}$

The 2 "D"s with a line above represent a SC stitch added above them.

SC in the next stitch and start a DC directly below it. Start a DC in the next 2 stitches. Finish by pulling through all 4 loops. Add a SC directly above the last DC.

(1 stitch will be skipped in the back)

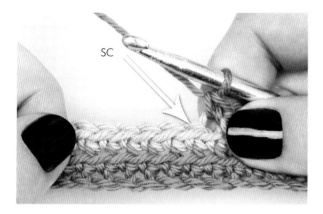

1. Start with a SC in the next stitch.

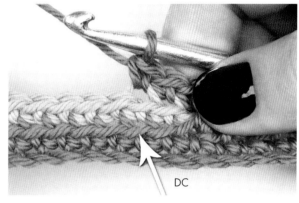

2. Begin adding a DC stitch directly below the SC. Work the stitch until you have 2 loops left on your hook.

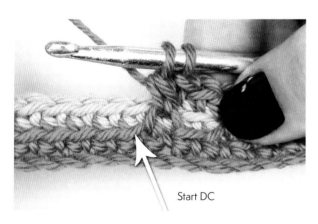

3. Yarn over and start your next DC in the next stitch, working the stitch until you have 3 loops left on your hook.

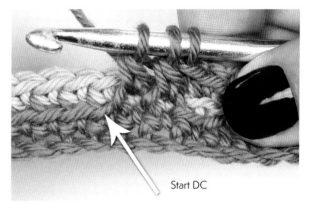

4. Yarn over and start your next DC in the next stitch, working the stitch until you have 4 loops left on your hook.

DC DECREASE 3 TOGETHER (continued)

5. Yarn over and pull through all 4 loops. This will connect all three DCs into one stitch.

6. Finish the sequence with a SC added directly above the last DC stitch.

DC Decrease 3 Together completed.

Left-Handed: Follow the same steps listed above.

DC DECREASE CENTERED

The 2 "D"s with a line above represent a SC stitch added above them.

SC in the next stitch and start a DC directly below the SC. Skip the next stitch. Start a DC in the following stitch. Finish by pulling through all 3 loops. Add a SC directly above the last DC stitch. **1 stitch will be skipped in the back.**

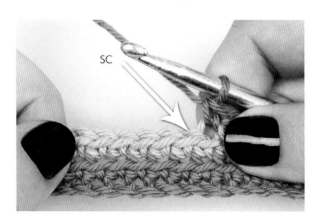

1. Start with a SC in the next stitch.

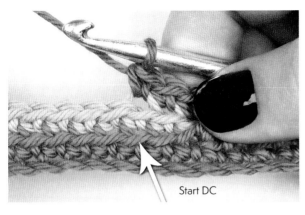

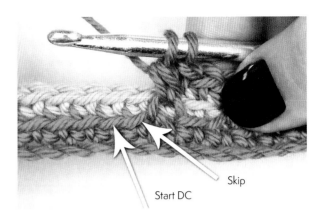

2. Begin adding a DC stitch directly below the SC. Work the stitch until you have 2 loops left on your hook.

3. Skip the next stitch. Yarn over and start your next DC in the following stitch, working the stitch until you have 3 loops left on your hook.

4. Yarn over and pull through all 3 loops. This will connect both DCs into one stitch.

5. Finish the sequence with a SC added directly above the last DC stitch.

DC Decrease Centered completed.

Left-Handed: Follow the same steps listed above.

TRIANGLES \ ▽ /

Skip the next stitch. Start with a DC in the following stitch. Add a SC directly above the DC. Add another DC back into the base of the first DC. Skip the next stitch.

(2 stitches will be skipped in the back)

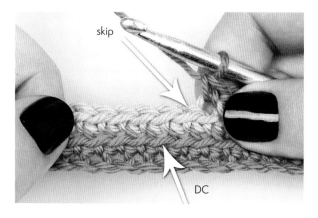

1. Skip the next stitch. Start with a DC in the next stitch.

2. Add a SC directly above the DC.

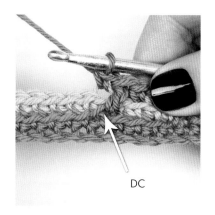

3. Add another DC back into the base of the first DC.

4. Skip the next stitch.

Triangle completed. **Image shows 1 SC after skip.**

Left-Handed: Follow the same steps listed above.

Stacked & Hidden Stitches

When you see stitches that are stacked on top of each other in a chart, and there isn't a blank box below, this indicates that the stitch to connect to will be partially hidden. In standard SC/DC mosaic crochet, overlay stitches are added into the front loop of the stitch in the row below, but when you're working with special stitches, the front loop of the stitch you're connecting to will be partially covered because it is part of a DC Decrease or Diagonal stitch. If you push the stitch over, you will be able to see the stitch to connect to. **Any stitches that are not stacked will be placed into a clearly visible stitch.**

DC OVER DIAGONAL

Hidden SC stitch in a diagonal.

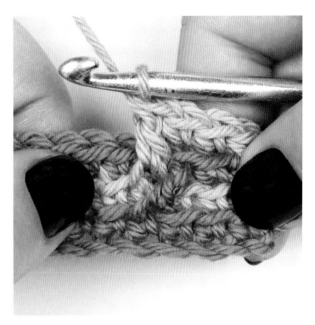

DC into the hidden SC stitch from the diagonal in the row below.

DIAGONAL OVER DIAGONAL

Two diagonal stitches stacked. The second diagonal is added to the hidden stitch from the diagonal in the row below.

DC OVER TRIANGLE

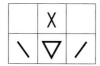

Hidden center stitch in a triangle.

DC added to hidden stitch in triangle.

TRIANGLE OVER TRIANGLE

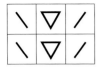

Triangles stacked. The next triangle is added to the hidden stitch in the triangle from the row below.

TWO DCS OVER DECREASE

Hidden stitch under the SC of a DC decrease.

Two DCs added to the hidden stitch in the DC Decrease. The top of the decrease is skipped.

DC DEC CENTERED OVER DC DEC 3 TOGETHER

$\overline{D}$	\	$\overline{D}$
$\overline{D}$	D	$\overline{D}$

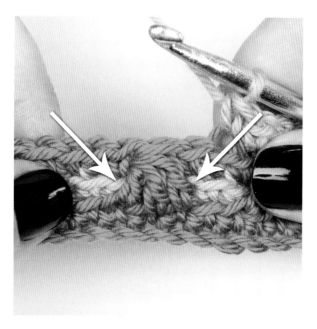

Hidden stitches under the SC stitches in a DC Decrease 3 Together. These are also the same hidden stitches in a DC Decrease Centered.

DC Decrease Centered, stacked on top of a DC Decrease 3 Together.

Special Stitch Combos

Some special stitches may seem a little tricky or confusing when you see them next to each other in a chart. This section shows examples of how some of these stitch combinations look side by side, so you can be sure each stitch is done correctly.

BACK-TO-BACK DIAGONALS

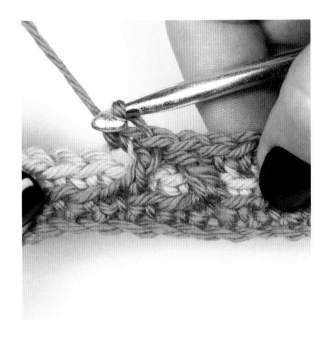

When a Diagonal Up ends and a Diagonal Down begins, you will have 2 stitches skipped in a row.

2 DC DECREASES IN A ROW

When you see 4 "D"s in a row, this does not mean 4 DCs are decreased together. These are 2 separate DC Decreases, one after the other.

This sequence starts with a SC for the first DC Decrease, then the next DC Decrease ends with a SC.

This sequence starts with a DC Decrease that ends with a SC, and the next DC Decrease starts with a SC, so there will be 2 SC stitches next to each other.

Acknowledgments

Ed & Jovie

Thank you both for encouraging me to fill our home with yarn, pillows and crazy ideas. During this whole book-writing process, I waited to hear that "oooh!" from both of you, so I would know a pattern was good enough to make it into the book. I sincerely value your honest opinions, and I'm grateful I get to spend my life with two dudes who are fine with me being completely immersed in crochet every day. Thank you for understanding why I ignore you while I'm counting stitches, and for giving me a free pass on cooking, cleaning and basic life stuff while I buried myself in patterns. We make a great team, and I love you both so much!

Mom & Dad

Thank you for being my biggest fans, and for never giving up on me. It's been a really rough road to get to where I am today, but you've always been on my side and I'm forever grateful for that. I know none of us could have imagined that crocheting would become the answer to any of my problems, but here we are! Thank you for believing in me. Love you!

Pattern Testers

I couldn't have done it without all of you! It was certainly a tough time of year to be testing patterns around the holidays, but you all came through and made it happen! I appreciate all of your feedback, suggestions and attention to detail, and I loved working with and getting to know all of you during this process! Thank you so much!

Page Street Publishing

Emily, I was so completely floored when you approached me with this incredible opportunity to write my own book that it didn't even really sink in right away. I wasn't sure if I should celebrate or wait a few days to be sure I wasn't just dreaming the whole thing! Writing a book has been a lifelong goal of mine, and I can't thank you enough for making it finally happen. You took a lot of risks by believing in me and my work, and by allowing me to be myself with all of my gothy designs! You and the whole team at Page Street have been so awesome to work with. I sincerely appreciate all the hard work that went on behind the scenes in order to create a book that just feels so "me"! You guys rock!

About the Author

Alexis Sixel is an artist who creates maximalist designs with saturated color, texture, patterns and drama. Passionate about interior design, modern art, fashion design and vintage style, she aims to inspire others to broaden their creative horizons. With over thirty years of crochet experience, Alexis has honed her skills to focus on mosaic crochet and teaching others this exciting technique.

Sixel Design was launched in 2020, and what started as just a hobby has blossomed into an extensive line of unique and edgy mosaic crochet patterns, ranging from Halloween for every day, to animal prints, geometric designs, florals and everything in between.

Born and raised in New York, Alexis currently lives in Maine with her husband, son and cat.

Website: www.sixeldesign.com
YouTube: @SixelDesign
Etsy: www.etsy.com/shop/sixelhome
Ravelry: www.ravelry.com/designers/alexis-sixel
Instagram: @sixeldesign
Facebook: /6LDesign

Index

S